1-2-3 Magic

Effective Discipline for Children 2-12

WORKBOOK

to Mrs. Wilson

1-2-3 Magic

Effective Discipline for Children 2-12

WORKBOOK

A User-Friendly Manual for America's #1 Child Discipline Program

Thomas W. Phelan, Ph.D.
Tracy M. Lewis, B.A.

Illustrations by Dan Farrell
Graphic Design by Mary Navolio
Distributed by Independent Publishers Group

Printed in the United States of America
10 9 8 7 6 5 4 3 2 1

For more information, contact:
ParentMagic, Inc.
800 Roosevelt Road
Glen Ellyn, Illinois 60137

Publisher's Cataloging-in-Publication
(Provided by Quality Books, Inc.)

Phelan, Thomas W., 1943-
    1-2-3 magic workbook / Thomas W. Phelan, Tracy M.
Lewis.
    p. cm.
    ISBN-13: 978-1-889140-44-5
    ISBN-10: 1-889140-44-9

    1. Discipline of children--Problems, exercises, etc.
2. Parenting--Problems, exercises, etc. 3. Child
rearing--Problems, exercises, etc.   I. Lewis, Tracy M.
II. Title. III. Title: One-two-three magic workbook.
IV. Title: 123 magic workbook.

HQ770.4.P44 2011   649'.64
                               QBI10-600246

Contents

Preface

This long-awaited *1-2-3 Magic Workbook* is a welcome addition to our *1-2-3 Magic* products. Based on the Fourth Edition of *1-2-3 Magic*, the *Workbook* takes parents through the program chapter by chapter in order to **maximize understanding** of the material, **encourage productive self-evaluation** and **promote the effective planning and execution** of *1-2-3 Magic* parenting strategies and interventions.

One of the chief objectives of all our *1-2-3 Magic* materials has always been simplicity, and that objective was especially critical in producing this *Workbook*. Those with experience in this field know that workbooks are usually intimidating pieces—fat, text-heavy, long and too often boring. We wanted to avoid that model at all costs. You will find the *1-2-3 Magic Workbook* to be user-friendly—**simple and easy to follow** but still thought-provoking and interesting. If *1-2-3 Magic* is America's simplest parenting program, the *1-2-3 Magic Workbook* is surely America's simplest parenting workbook.

Who Can Use the New *1-2-3 Magic Workbook*?

Parents (including foster and adoptive) and other direct caretakers (grandparents, teachers, preschool and after school staffs) can use the *1-2-3 Magic Workbook* to improve their disciplinary effectiveness and adult/child relationship skills. After watching the *1-2-3 Magic* DVDs, listening to the CDs, or reading the book, some parents will want to work their way through the entire *Workbook*, chapter by chapter. They can then begin to apply each new skill.

Mental health professionals, pediatricians and other auxiliary staff can also use the *Workbook* to guide the training of parents in *1-2-3 Magic*. Once again, after doing the DVDs, CDs or book, some folks might want to go right through the entire *Workbook* to make absolutely sure they're doing things right. Others might decide they only need certain parts of the *Workbook*; they might review those parts when they are having particular difficulties. For example, those struggling with testing and manipulation might want to do Chapter 10—from beginning to end—before they go back to try their new methods again with their children.

The *1-2-3 Magic Workbook* can be used as a **training guide for one-on-one clinical sessions** with individual families, but it can also serve as a structure for one- to two-hour group therapy/training sessions with multiple families. Chapter sections such as *Questions About Content, What Would You Suggest?, How Are Things at Your House?, Putting 1-2-3 Magic Into Action with Your Family* and *Troubleshooting* provide an excellent basis for productive and provocative group discussions.

Two Main Sections

The *1-2-3 Magic Workbook* has two main sections. In **Section I we deal with each chapter of the *1-2-3 Magic Fourth Edition***, breaking the treatment of the material down into seven parts:

1. Overview of Content
2. Questions for Reflection/Discussion
3. Case Study
4. What Would You Suggest? Solutions for the Case Study
5. How Are Things at Your House? Self-Evaluation
6. Putting *1-2-3 Magic* Into Action with Your Family
7. Troubleshooting
8. Wrap-Up

In Section II we present illustrated, comic-type stories that show how real parents actually applied *1-2-3 Magic* strategies. The true stories are entertaining and engaging, and they include further questions for reflection and discussion.

Whether you are a parent, mental health professional or both, we hope the *1-2-3 Magic Workbook* provides you with valuable assistance in applying **America's most popular child discipline program.**

1

I felt like I was drowning.

Then one day an old high school friend flew in for my birthday. She would soon be the best birthday gift I ever got.

After Sally saw what was happening at my house, she told me her story.

Several years back, her two kids had been running **her** house.

Then she and her husband came across a parenting program with a strange name.

IT WAS CALLED *1-2-3 MAGIC*. WE GOT THE BOOK AND DVD.

!?

The program was simple and easy to learn. They mastered it in just a few hours.

LOOK AT THIS!

YEP, THAT'S US.

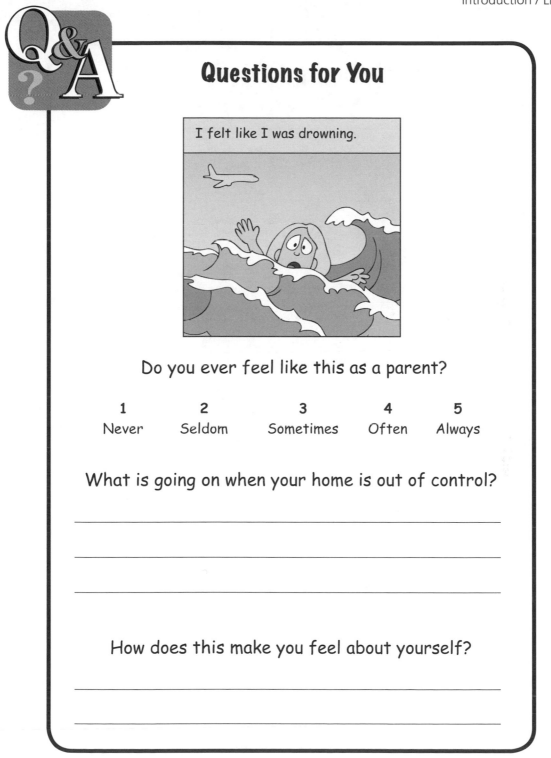

Q&A

Questions for You

I felt like I was drowning.

Do you ever feel like this as a parent?

1	2	3	4	5
Never	Seldom	Sometimes	Often	Always

What is going on when your home is out of control?

_____

_____

_____

How does this make you feel about yourself?

_____

_____

Friendly Advice?

Some parents suggested spanking, but I didn't like that idea.

DON'T PUT UP WITH THAT GARBAGE. CRACK DOWN!

Did Lisa need to "crack down"?

_____

_____

_____

Does cracking down have to mean
physical discipline?

_____

_____

Friendly Advice?

Other parents told me I needed to explain more, but the kids didn't seem to care what I said.

THE REASON YOU CAN'T...

YEAH, YEAH, YEAH...

Are explanations helpful with your kids in discipline situations?

When do you think explanations are absolutely necessary?

Attitude Adjustment Part I: The Kids

How did Lisa's son feel at this point about the
transformation in his mother?
Did he cooperate willingly with the change?

_____

_____

How did the boy feel at the end? _____

Attitude Adjustment Part II: The Parent

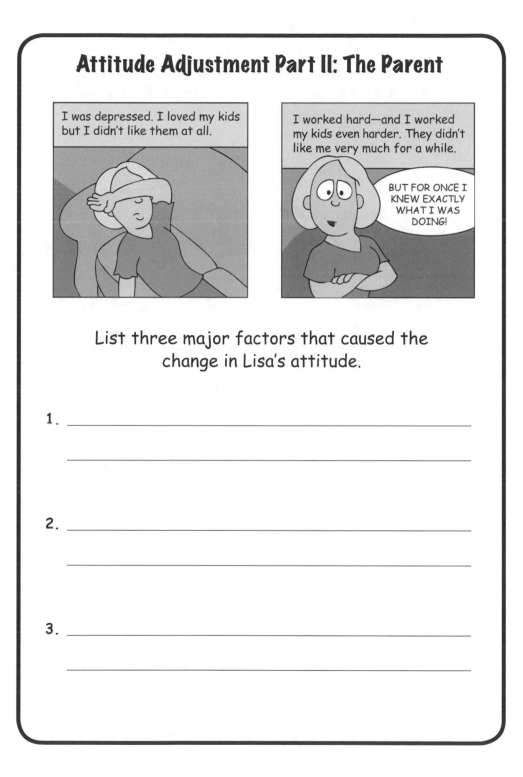

List three major factors that caused the change in Lisa's attitude.

1. _____

_____

2. _____

_____

3. _____

_____

1
The Parenting Profession

Chapter Overview

Children do not enter the world with instructions. After the initial excitement of bringing your new baby home, you may begin wishing kids did have a "How To Raise Me" manual. In this chapter you will learn some of the basics you will need to raise happy and confident kids. You will learn how to begin with the right perspective and how to examine your automatic parenting responses. In addition, you will find out what to expect when you begin *1-2-3 Magic* with your children.

Questions About Chapter 1

1. What are the two most important qualities of effective parents?
2. When is your automatic response to your child a good thing?
3. When should you replace an automatic response?
4. How should you start the *1-2-3 Magic* program?
5. What are the two possible responses from your child when you begin the 1-2-3 plan?

Case Study

Jill loves her kids. She has eight-year-old Michael and four-year-old Kennedy. Jill loves to read to them before bed and play board games with them. However, Jill is having some trouble with her kids. Michael teases Kennedy non-stop, and going to the store with the kids is disastrous. Jill and her husband have talked with Michael about how he should treat his sister, but Michael continues aggravating Kennedy. The store issue is not getting any better. Lately, Jill has just bought the kids candy and toys when they go shopping to keep them quiet.

What Would You Suggest?

1. Based on chapter one, what is Jill doing right?

_____

_____

_____

2. Where can Jill improve?

_____

_____

_____

_____

_____

Key Concept

Research has shown that effective parents are warm and friendly on the one hand, but also demanding and firm on the other. Both orientations are critical to raising emotionally intelligent and mature kids.

How Are Things at Your House?

Rate yourself on a scale of 1 to 5 in the following parenting areas. 1 means NOT SO GOOD and 5 means FANTASTIC.

NOT SO GOOD			FANTASTIC	
1	**2**	**3**	**4**	**5**

Warm and Friendly _____   Positive Automatic Responses _____

Demanding and Firm _____   Negative Automatic Responses _____

Putting *1-2-3 Magic* Into Action with Your Family

Now it's time to start putting what you've learned so far into action. Here are some questions and exercises to help you begin making plans for dealing with your children.

1. Which negative automatic responses do you need to replace with more deliberate, respectful actions?

   _____

   _____

   _____

2. Think about your children. Do you think they will be "immediate cooperators" or "immediate testers"?

   _____

   _____

   _____

Troubleshooting Exercise

Automatic responses are tough to change because they are—well … automatic. Think about the times when you have had some negative automatic responses. Describe some of them here and take note of when they happened. Knowing when they happen will be helpful when you begin to replace these negative times with a more positive parental approach.

Chapter Wrap-Up

- Parents should be both warm/friendly and demanding/firm.

- Positive automatic parenting habits should be maintained.

- Negative parenting habits should be replaced with deliberate and respectful strategies.

- Kids will fall into either the "immediate cooperator" or "immediate tester" category once the *1-2-3 Magic* plan is implemented.

2
Your Three Parenting Jobs

Chapter Overview

Parenting can be an overwhelming task. Whining, tantrums, homework and getting kids to bed are just a few of the many chores to be done. This chapter will simplify the work of parenting into three basic jobs. The first job involves controlling obnoxious behavior. In this step you will learn to **"Stop"** negative behavior like screaming and whining. Job #2 involves encouraging good behavior. We call this **"Start"** behavior since it deals with getting your child to do things like homework and room cleaning. The last important job focuses on **strengthening your relationship** with your child.

Questions About Chapter 2

1. What are the three parenting jobs?
2. What is the difference between "Start" and "Stop" behavior?
3. What are some examples of "Stop" and "Start" behavior?
4. Which kind of behavior requires more motivation?
5. What are the benefits of strengthening your bond with the kids?

Case Study

Mary is very frustrated and is having a difficult time with her eight-year-old son, John. Every night has turned into a battle. When Mary tells John it's time to start his homework, an argument occurs. John yells and throws a tantrum. Mary usually gets upset too. In addition, John is continually making his younger sister, Abby, cry by saying mean things to her. Mary loves John but is just tired and worn-out from John's problem behavior at night. She desperately would like more peaceful evenings with her children.

What Would You Suggest?

1. Identify the Stop behavior and the Start behavior problems that Mary needs to deal with.

    _____

    _____

    _____

2. According to this chapter, what should Mary use to address Stop behavior and what should she use for Start behavior?

    _____

    _____

    _____

Quik Tip
Exactly how you start depends on how much energy you have. If you feel like you're barely hanging on by your fingernails, you might want to start with only counting. Then add the good behavior and relationship steps after the kids know you mean business.

How Are Things at Your House?

Rate yourself on a scale of 1 to 5 in the following parenting areas.

NOT SO GOOD	FANTASTIC
1 2 3	4 5

How are you doing currently with Stop behaviors
(screaming, whining, tantrums, etc.)?   **Rate:** _____

How are you doing with Start behaviors
(going to bed, homework, getting up in the morning, etc.)?   **Rate:** _____

Putting *1-2-3 Magic* Into Action with Your Family

1. Remember that Stop behaviors are those actions your child does that you want them to stop doing. (e.g., whining, complaining, etc.) Make a list of Stop behaviors you would like to address with your child. If you have more than one child, make a list for each.

2. Remember that Start behaviors are those actions you would like your child to begin doing (e.g., doing homework, going to bed, etc.). Make a list of those Start behaviors you would like to see your child begin without a fight. If you have more than one child, make a list for each.

_____   _____

_____   _____

_____   _____

_____   _____

_____   _____

Troubleshooting Exercise

Since counting is so easy, one of the biggest problems we encounter is parents' using counting for Start behavior. For the behaviors below, check the Stop behaviors that you should count.

☐ Cleaning rooms

☐ Arguing with a sibling

☐ Not eating vegetables

☐ Whining in the car

☐ Begging for candy at the store

☐ Going to bed on time

☐ Not practicing a musical instrument

☐ Throwing a football in the house

☐ Refusing to come inside when asked

☐ Leaving shoes all over the house

Chapter Wrap-Up

- There are three basic jobs of parenting: controlling obnoxious behavior, encouraging good behavior and strengthening your relationship with your child.

- Counting is for Stop behavior.

- Encouraging good behavior requires more motivation in the kids.

- A good relationship with your child makes parenting easier and more fun.

3

The Little Adult Assumption

Chapter Overview

Many parents carry around in their heads a trouble-producing notion that causes discipline attempts that fail. This idea is known as the "Little Adult Assumption" and this assumption often causes stormy scenes that can even lead to physical child abuse. Parents with this idea rely too heavily on words and reasoning. This chapter challenges the Little Adult Assumption and provides an alternative view of kids and parenting. In addition, you will begin to understand the overall orientation of *1-2-3 Magic* as you learn about the notion of "dictatorship to democracy."

Questions About Chapter 3

1. What is the Little Adult Assumption?

2. What do adults who believe the Little Adult Assumption rely on in dealing with their kids?

3. What is one big danger in relying heavily on words and reasoning for disciplining children?

4. What does "dictatorship to democracy" mean?

5. What is one fear that many parents have that can negatively affect their parenting?

Case Study

Tyler, Linda's six-year-old son, always wants to stay up with is older brother, Trevor, who is fifteen. Tyler's bedtime is at 8:30 and Trevor usually goes to bed about 10 o'clock. Every night when Linda tries to put Tyler to bed, he doesn't want to go. Linda usually begins by calmly explaining to Tyler why his brother gets to stay up later. Tyler usually argues with his mother, getting her upset. The conflict often escalates with Tyler's father intervening and spanking Tyler. Linda desperately wants a calmer bedtime ritual with her son, but doesn't know what to do.

What Would You Suggest?

1. What are the two main problems you see in the story above?

_____

_____

2. What is the first thing Linda needs to do?

_____

_____

_____

CAUTION
One explanation, if really necessary, is fine. It's the attempts at *repeated explanations* that get adults and kids into trouble. Too much parent talking irritates and distracts children.

How Are Things at Your House?

Rate yourself on a scale of 1 to 5 in the following parenting areas.

NOT SO GOOD				FANTASTIC
1	2	3	4	5

Talking too much during discipline situations   **Rate:** _____

_____

How well is your parenting going using the Little Adult Assumption? **Rate:** _____

Explain. _____

_____

_____

Putting *1-2-3 Magic* Into Action with Your Family

1. Understanding the Little Adult Assumption is the key to understanding how to apply *1-2-3 Magic*. In your own words, write a description of what the Little Adult Assumption means.

_____

_____

_____

_____

2. How easy will it be for you to switch from explaining to training your kids?

_____

_____

_____

Troubleshooting Exercise

Take a moment and list those times when you are most likely to operate with the Little Adult Assumption (bedtime, at the store, after-school, etc.).

_____   _____

_____   _____

_____   _____

_____   _____

_____   _____

Chapter Wrap-Up

- The Little Adult Assumption is the cause of most discipline mistakes.
- Parents often rely too heavily on words and reasoning.
- Parents should begin as benevolent dictators and gradually move toward a more democratic parenting style.

4
The Two Biggest Discipline Mistakes

Chapter Overview

The two biggest mistakes that parents make in dealing with children are these: **Too Much Talking** and **Too Much Emotion**. While too much talking can irritate and distract kids, too much emotion can be even more destructive. It can result in adult outbursts and actions that parents regret. When it comes to discipline, you want to be consistent, decisive and calm. This chapter analyzes why kids sometimes seem to want their parents upset, and how parents can keep themselves quiet and under control.

Questions About Chapter 4

1. Why does Too Much Talking make kids less likely to cooperate?

2. What is a possible reward for a child if he gets his parents upset?

3. What are three important guidelines for discipline?

4. What are the two important rules in applying the *1-2-3 Magic* plan?

5. What are some ways that some parents remind themselves about the "No-Talking" and "No-Emotion" rules?

Case Study

Amy's two-year-old son, Matthew, is whining all the time. No matter how much attention Amy gives Matthew, he continues whining when he wants something. Amy has told him over and over not to whine. She's also tried giving Matthew extra attention. Nothing seems to work. Lately, she's been getting upset and yelling at him because she is so frustrated. Amy feels guilty for her explosions, but she just doesn't know what to do.

What Would You Suggest?

Based on Chapter 4, what are some of the problems you see in the story above?

_____

_____

_____

What is the first thing Amy needs to realize?

_____

_____

Quik Tip

If your little child can get big old you all upset, your upset is the big splash for him. Your emotional outburst accidentally makes your child feel powerful. It's just a normal childhood feeling: Having all that power temporarily rewards—or feels good to—the inferior part of the child.

How Are Things at Your House

Rate yourself on a scale of 1 to 5 in the following parenting areas.

NOT SO GOOD ···································· FANTASTIC

| 1 | 2 | 3 | 4 | 5 |

Talking too much **Rate:** _____

Getting too upset **Rate:** _____

If you rated yourself below a 5, what are some ways you can improve?

_____

_____

_____

_____

Putting *1-2-3 Magic* Into Action with Your Family

1. How can you show more positive emotions such as affection and praise to your child?

_____

_____

_____

2. What are some ways your child gets you upset?
How will you counteract his attempts in the future?

_____

_____

_____

Troubleshooting Exercise

Following the No-Talking and No-Emotion rules can be challenging for some parents. In the heat of battle, how will you remind yourself not to talk or get upset?

_____

_____

_____

_____

Chapter Wrap-Up

- Express your emotion toward your child when it is positive.

- Too much talking interferes with discipline.

- Too much emotion can lead to adult emotional outbursts and can reinforce bad behavior.

**Too Much Talking
Too Much Emotion**

5
Counting: Simple But Not Easy!

Chapter Overview

This chapter will show you the "nuts and bolts" of controlling obnoxious behavior. The 1-2-3 method will help you regain control and it will help your kids take more responsibility for their own behavior. This method will not be difficult for you to learn. It is straightforward and easy for both you and your children to understand. The part that can be a little tough is remembering to keep away from the two big parenting mistakes—too much talking and too much emotion!

Remember: Excessive parental chattering and emotional outbursts will ruin any discipline program!

Questions About Chapter 5

1. How is the 1-2-3 method "simple but not always easy"?
2. How long do you wait between counts?
3. What happens after your child comes out of time-out?
4. What is an "automatic 3"?
5. Give some examples of time-out alternatives.

Case Study

Tom's daughter, Tina, has thrown a huge temper tantrum because she wanted to go outside and play after her father had told her that it was time to do her homework. Tom told her "No," and the screaming and badgering began. Tom counted Tina, got to three, and sent her to time-out for seven minutes. Tom was furious at her for having been so difficult to deal with. Now the seven-minute time-out is over, and Tina comes out of her room and goes directly to her father for a hug. Tom is still angry with her and wants to sit her down and tell her how things are going to be from now on.

What Would You Suggest?

1. Is Tom on the right track? Should he speak to Tina about her behavior right after she has completed her time-out?

_____

_____

_____

2. Give an example of an appropriate way that you would interact with Tina after her time-out. What would you say to her?

_____

_____

_____

How Are Things at Your House?

1. Think about the primary disciplinarians in your child's life. Who is the most likely to have trouble with the No-Talking rule?

   _____

2. Who will have the most trouble with the No-Emotion rule?

   _____

Putting *1-2-3 Magic* Into Action with Your Family

Think of your children one at a time. Given what you know about them, who is probably going to have the most trouble handling the new law of the land?

_____

_____

_____

_____

_____

Key Concept
Talk too much and you switch your child's focus off the need for good behavior and on to the possibility of an enjoyable argument. There are plenty of kids who would rather cut off their left leg than lose a good battle of words.

Troubleshooting Exercise

There may be times when your children decide to be very stubborn and not willingly retreat to their time-out areas. For each of your children, make a list of three time-out alternatives that you could use. The list may be the same or different for each of your children.

_____   _____

_____   _____

_____   _____

_____   _____

_____   _____

_____   _____

Chapter Wrap-Up

- There are several benefits to counting. Less stress for you, short punishments for the kids and more time for fun for everyone!

- The No-Talking and No-Emotion rules are vital to the success of the counting method.

6
Frequently Asked Questions

Chapter Overview

This chapter is full of answers to many questions that parents have regarding how to apply the 1-2-3 method. By this time, in fact, you have probably thought of at least a half dozen of these questions yourself! Read Chapter 6 carefully and apply the principles. This preparation will help you not be caught by surprise every time your children do not cooperate perfectly. You will soon see improved behavior from your kids, and you will be able to enjoy them a lot more!

Questions About Chapter 6

1. What are some challenges that may present themselves when you try to use a "time-out chair" instead of a room?

2. What type of grandparents do you have to deal with?

3. How do you apply the 1-2-3 when the phone rings?

4. What should you do if your child doesn't want to come out of time-out when his or her time is up?

5. Does being counted affect a child's self-esteem in a positive or negative way?

Case Study

Jack's four-year-old son, Ethan, can be quite a handful. Ethan gets very upset when he gets counted and gets to a count of 3. Today Ethan is attempting to grab a toy from his older brother. Jack counts him in an attempt to get him to let go of the toy. He does not let go and gets to a count of 3. Ethan does not voluntarily go to his room, so Jack has to carry him there. Now Ethan is coming out repeatedly and refusing to stay put for his time-out.

What Would You Suggest?

1. List three things that Jack can do to ensure that Ethan stays in his room.

_____

_____

_____

2. Which of these three methods would you choose to try first?

_____

How Are Things at Your House?

1. Which questions were most helpful to you in chapter 6?

_____

_____

_____

2. Do you have any questions that have not yet been answered?

_____

_____

_____

_____

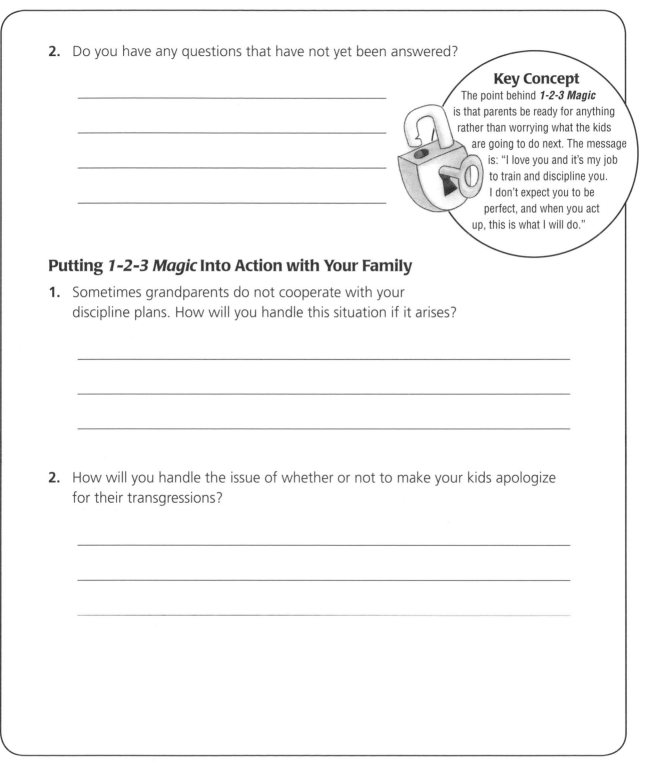

Key Concept

The point behind *1-2-3 Magic* is that parents be ready for anything rather than worrying what the kids are going to do next. The message is: "I love you and it's my job to train and discipline you. I don't expect you to be perfect, and when you act up, this is what I will do."

Putting *1-2-3 Magic* Into Action with Your Family

1. Sometimes grandparents do not cooperate with your discipline plans. How will you handle this situation if it arises?

_____

_____

_____

2. How will you handle the issue of whether or not to make your kids apologize for their transgressions?

_____

_____

_____

Troubleshooting Exercise

Before you begin using *1-2-3 Magic*, go through Chapter 6 very carefully and find the difficult issues that you think may apply to each of your children. Creating a plan prior to needing one will help you tremendously.

_____

_____

_____

_____

_____

_____

_____

_____

Keep in mind that every child is different. Some children react beautifully to starting the 1-2-3 method of discipline while others do a lot of testing. Respect your child's individuality and find the solutions that work for your family.

Chapter Wrap-Up

Most common situations related to the 1-2-3 discipline plan have easy solutions.

Keep the book handy so you can refer back to it often.

7
Out in Public

Chapter Overview

Being in public presents its own special problems. When our kids choose to challenge us out there in the big, bad world, we sometimes have to deal with our own red-hot embarrassment, which causes us to become far more frazzled than we would be at home. Additionally, we have to contend with logistical issues involving the time-out. Chapter 7 deals with these situations. If we can formulate a plan before these circumstances arise, it makes it easier to handle them when they do.

Questions About Chapter 7

1. What is so difficult about handling challenging behavior in public?

2. What are some examples of time-out places that you can use in public?

3. Why do you give four counts with the "1-2-3-4"?

4. How can you handle difficult behavior in the car?

5. What is the most important thing to remember about long car trips?

Case Study

Jan is walking through the grocery store with her three-year-old son, Billy. They enter the snack aisle and Billy immediately homes in on the chocolate chip cookies. He attempts to grab them from the shelf and Jan tells him to stop. He looks at his mother, digs in his heels and yells, "But I WANT the cookies!!!!!" Again Jan tells Billy that he can't have the cookies, but that she will be happy to give him the crackers that she brought from home instead. Billy throws himself onto the floor, right there in aisle five, and screams as though someone were assaulting him.

What Would You Suggest?

1. Identify the Stop behavior that Billy is presenting.

_____

_____

2. What specific first step should Jan take to stop this behavior?

_____

_____

3. Name one time-out spot that Jan could use in this situation.

_____

_____

_____

Quik Tip

When you're out in public, there is always either a room, something like a room or a symbolic location where a time-out can be served. And don't forget your time-out alternatives. Just because people are watching does not mean that you have to be at your kids' mercy!

How Are Things at Your House?

On a scale from 1 to 5 (with 1 meaning that your child's behavior in public is generally AWFUL and 5 meaning there are NO PROBLEMS), rate your child's behavior.

AWFUL ···································· **NO PROBLEMS**

| 1 | 2 | 3 | 4 | 5 |

1. How does your child behave in public?
   (If you have more than one child, do this for each one.)

   Rate: _____   **Rate:** _____   **Rate:** _____   **Rate:** _____

2. Now do the same for your child's behavior during car trips.

   Rate: _____   **Rate:** _____   **Rate:** _____   **Rate:** _____

Putting *1-2-3 Magic* Into Action with Your Family

1. Using what you learned in Chapter 7, describe how you will now handle temper tantrums in public.

   _____

   _____

2. How will you handle misbehavior in the car?

   _____

   _____

Troubleshooting Exercises

1. Put on your thinking cap before you go out into the world with the kids! Write down three things that you can do to make your time in public easier and more fun for you and your children.

    _____

    _____

    _____

2. How have you handled problem behavior in public with your children in the past? Has this been effective?

    _____

    _____

    _____

Chapter Wrap-Up

- **Remember that time-out doesn't have to occur in your child's room.**
  Be creative and you can probably come up with a suitable time-out spot when you are out and about.

- **Fight your mortification at your child's public temper tantrums.**
  All parents have been there and most have nothing but sympathy for your difficult moment. The people who haven't been there don't understand anyway, so don't worry about what they think!

8
Sibling Rivalry, Tantrums and Pouting

Chapter Overview

There are some situations that require minor modifications of the 1-2-3. What do you do when your kids are fighting and you have no idea who the main culprit is? What do you do when the time-out period is over, but your daughter is still throwing a major tantrum in her room? And what about pouting? Your son isn't really making any noise, but he's definitely trying to push your buttons with his whole "woe is me" routine! Sibling rivalry, tantrums and pouting are covered here in this chapter.

Questions About Chapter 8

1. When your children are fighting, how do you know who gets counted?

2. What are the two stupid questions that a parent should never ask fighting children?

3. What should you do if both fighting children share a room and they receive a count of 3?

4. What happens if you send a child to time-out and her tantrum continues?

5. How should a parent handle pouting?

Case Study

Theresa's daughter, Jennifer, was angry because she didn't get the cookies she asked for. She was feeling very sorry for herself, sitting on the couch with her arms crossed and a pouty look on her face. Theresa was mildly amused but didn't show it. She walked into the kitchen. Jennifer decided to follow. What good is being upset if there is no one around to notice it? What Theresa had thought was a little funny a few minutes before was now becoming quite irritating. Being followed around by an actively unhappy youngster was not funny at all!

What Would You Suggest?

1. What kind of pouting is Jennifer engaging in?

_____

2. If you were Theresa, how would you handle this situation?

_____

_____

_____

CAUTION
Never ask the world's two stupidest questions, "Who started it?" and "What happened?" unless you think someone is physically injured. Do you expect your kids to come up with George Washington's version of "I cannot tell a lie"?

How Are Things at Your House?

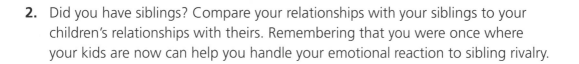

1. Think of your children one at a time. Does one of your children tend to bully the others? Perhaps you have a child who is a perpetual victim (in his own mind!) and a bit of a tattletale. Discuss how either of these dynamics might come into play and how you would manage them.

_____

_____

_____

2. Did you have siblings? Compare your relationships with your siblings to your children's relationships with theirs. Remembering that you were once where your kids are now can help you handle your emotional reaction to sibling rivalry.

_____

_____

_____

Putting *1-2-3 Magic* Into Action with Your Family

1. Using what you learned in Chapter 8, describe what you will do differently (if anything) when dealing with sibling rivalry.

_____

_____

_____

2. If your children share a room, make a short list of alternative time-out locations for one of them to use in the event of a time-out for both of them due to fighting.

_____   _____

_____   _____

_____   _____

Troubleshooting Exercise

Your child is passively pouting and it's getting on your nerves. What can you do, since counting isn't recommended as a first option? Thinking this out ahead of time can help you stay calm when the situation arises.

_____

_____

_____

Chapter Wrap-Up

- Remember that there is nothing that you can do that will put a permanent end to sibling rivalry. Live with it and manage it as best you can.

- Pouting is ignored unless the child becomes an aggressive pouter.

- With kids four and older, time-out doesn't start until the temper tantrum ends!

9
Getting Started with Counting

Chapter Overview

Congratulations! You are ready to begin the *1-2-3 Magic* program in earnest.
Do you just start throwing numbers around and hope for the best? No! Now it's
time to let your precious progeny in on what's about to happen in all your lives.
What you need to do is to have a short conversation with your kids explaining the
nuts and bolts of counting. More importantly, let them know how this is going to
improve all your lives immeasurably. Won't they be surprised!

Questions About Chapter 9

1. About how long should the Kickoff Conversation last?

2. What is the best way to handle this conversation for parents who live apart?

3. What part of the 1-2-3 program do you tell your kids that they will actually like?

4. Do you think the kids will believe you are serious?

5. How will you manage any questions the children have?

Case Study

Jim and Michelle decide to sit their children down and tell them about *1-2-3 Magic*. Their twelve-year-old daughter, Taylor, responds with sarcastic laughter and their ten-year-old son, John, responds with, "This is so stupid!"

What Would You Suggest?

If you are Jim and Michelle, how do you respond to your kids' attitudes?

_____

_____

_____

How Are Things at Your House?

Do either you or your partner have trouble with the No-Talking rule? If so, be aware of this. Use the lines below to come up with a short and sweet start to your Kickoff Conversation.

_____

_____

_____

_____

_____

Putting *1-2-3 Magic* Into Action with Your Family

If you have a child that is two or three years old, how can you explain the 1-2-3 method to her?

_____

_____

_____

_____

How will you explain counting to a ten-year-old?

_____

_____

_____

Quik Tip

It's very important to rehearse or role-play the counting procedure, for little kids as well as older children. This gives the children a real feel for what's going to happen and it also lets them know you're serious.

_____

_____

_____

Troubleshooting Exercise

Remember that your kids will probably not jump up and hug you for deciding to bring *1-2-3 Magic* into their lives. Keep your expectations realistic and when in doubt, count.

What will you do if your nine-year-old son says "This is dumb and all our friends think you guys are weird!"?

_____

_____

_____

Chapter Wrap-Up

You've learned the 1-2-3 method, you've had most of your questions answered and you alerted your offspring to what lies ahead. Now it's time to get started!

**You're almost ready to begin your first
giant parenting step:**

Controlling Obnoxious Behavior!

10
The Six Kinds of Testing and Manipulation

Chapter Overview

When you begin *1-2-3 Magic*, there are actually some children who will be immediate cooperators. They will understand the new rules quickly and will comply with the time-outs that you give. In fact, these are the kids who will rarely ever get to a count of three. Our guess is that the immediate cooperator in your house, if there is one, isn't the reason that you purchased this book! There is probably another child (or two!) who is not going to be happy with all this new stuff that you're introducing. Welcome to testing and manipulation!

Questions About Chapter 10

1. List the Six Kinds of Testing and Manipulation.

2. What is the one kind of testing and manipulation that does NOT get counted?

3. Why is it bad if your child has a favorite tactic?

4. What is the easiest but worst way to get a child to stop testing and manipulating?

5. What is a "4-1" testing pattern?

Case Study

The Lopez family had a kickoff conversation with their kids two days ago. Today, their eleven-year-old-son, Juan, asks his father, Marc, if he can spend the night with a friend. It's a Tuesday in February. Marc tells Juan that he can't spend the night with his friend because they have a rule about not having sleepovers on school nights. Juan becomes very angry. He picks up a book that is sitting on his dad's desk and forcefully throws it to the floor.

What Would You Suggest?

1. Identify the testing tactic that Juan is using in the scenario above.

_____

2. What is the best course of action for Marc to take with Juan right now?

_____

How Are Things at Your House?

1. Think of your children one at a time. Currently, what is the favored testing tactic that each of your children uses?

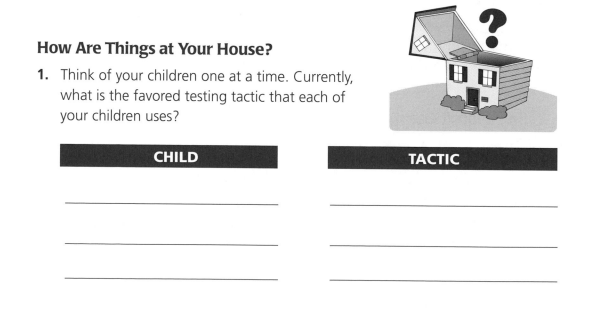

CHILD	TACTIC
_____	_____
_____	_____
_____	_____

2. What does this mean for you and your discipline?

_____

_____

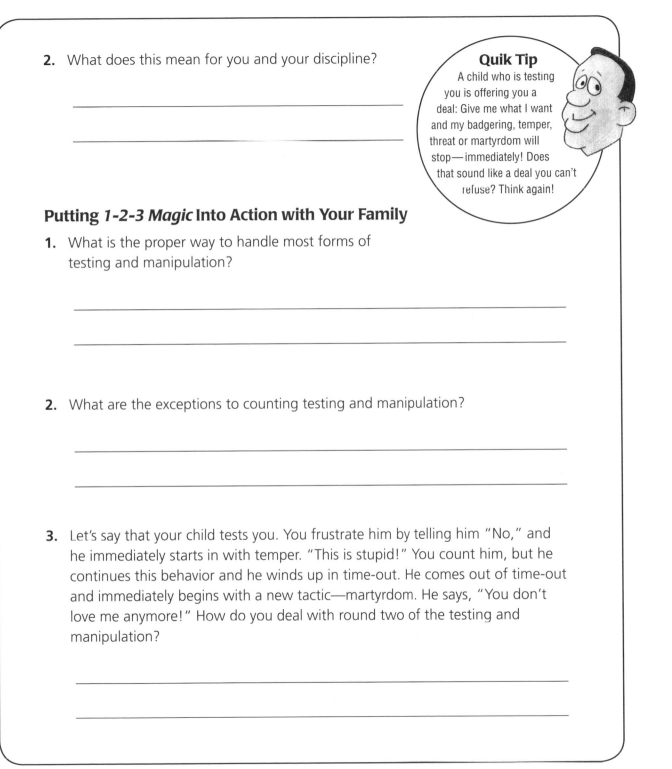

Quik Tip

A child who is testing you is offering you a deal: Give me what I want and my badgering, temper, threat or martyrdom will stop—immediately! Does that sound like a deal you can't refuse? Think again!

Putting *1-2-3 Magic* Into Action with Your Family

1. What is the proper way to handle most forms of testing and manipulation?

_____

_____

2. What are the exceptions to counting testing and manipulation?

_____

_____

3. Let's say that your child tests you. You frustrate him by telling him "No," and he immediately starts in with temper. "This is stupid!" You count him, but he continues this behavior and he winds up in time-out. He comes out of time-out and immediately begins with a new tactic—martyrdom. He says, "You don't love me anymore!" How do you deal with round two of the testing and manipulation?

_____

_____

Troubleshooting Exercises

1. When your child begins to test you, in the beginning of the ordeal, it can be easy to keep your cool. However, some kids are masters and keep on and on and on, even after you send them to time-out! Some kids know that if they keep on long enough, they can make you break! One of the worst things you can do with testing and manipulation is to keep your cool for a long period of time *and then lose it!* Come up with a short list of things you can do to help you remain calm under these circumstances.

_____   _____

_____   _____

_____   _____

2. Keep in mind that some children will jump from tactic to tactic if one isn't working for them. As frustrating as this is, it means that you are doing well! Try to remember this and it should help ease your frustration during the first difficult days.

Chapter Wrap-Up

The Six Kinds of Testing and Manipulation: badgering, temper, threat, martyrdom, butter up and physical tactics.

***Keep in mind that a child who is testing is doing it out of frustration.
Testing won't last forever—if you handle it correctly!***

Key Concept
The first goal of testing is for the child to get what he wants. Since he's less powerful than you are, he must use some emotional manipulation. If the child still fails to get what he wants, the second goal of testing is often retaliation or revenge. The kid is going to make you pay!

11
Counting in Action

Chapter Overview

This chapter provides some real-life scenarios involving different adults using *1-2-3 Magic*. This will give you a feel for how counting should work and what some of the pitfalls may be. We'll also show you, however, how to climb out of the pits you may fall into! These examples will demonstrate how it happens that we sometimes allow ourselves to get overly chatty or emotional. The examples will also demonstrate how to stay on your toes and avoid those mistakes.

Questions About Chapter 11

1. In most instances, what is the best way to handle a problem between siblings?

2. What question should you never ask two fighting siblings?

3. We aren't supposed to use counting with a child who has been told to go to bed and doesn't. Why not?

4. In the "Dog Teasing" scenario in this chapter, mom has to physically escort the child to time-out. What if your child is almost your size and refuses to go? What do you do?

5. Under the section in the chapter labeled "Requests," Tom's mother added five minutes to his ten-minute time-out. Why?

Case Study

Your daughters are in their shared bedroom playing with their dolls together. You haven't heard what has led up to this, but suddenly you hear yelling coming from the room. Both girls are screaming at the tops of their lungs! You walk into the room and they are playing tug of war with a doll's dress.

What Would You Suggest?

1. Who do you count?

   _____

2. If the kids get to three, how do you handle the time-out? Remember, they share a bedroom.

   _____

   _____

   _____

3. How should parents handle their own personal frustration with sibling rivalry?

   _____

   _____

   _____

How Are Things at Your House?

1. What is one of the main reasons that parents have such a hard time disciplining in public?

_____

_____

2. How can you address this? Write down a few things that you can tell yourself in public that will help you to get beyond this.

_____

_____

_____

Putting *1-2-3 Magic* Into Action with Your Family

1. How do you handle problems that arise with your child's behavior when he has friends over to play?

_____

_____

_____

2. Which of your children gives you the most trouble out in public? List a few ways you can prepare yourself (and your child!) before you even leave the house.

_____

_____

_____

Troubleshooting Exercises

1. It's very easy to allow our own frustrations and bad moods to affect our parenting, even when our moods have nothing at all to do with our children. Be aware of this fact and try very hard to keep a cool head when disciplining, even when you'd rather blow up.

2. Sometimes we go backwards, even when we've been using _1-2-3 Magic_ for quite awhile. How do you recover after you've slipped up in front of your kids? What do you do if you find yourself screaming at one of them instead of calmly counting?

_____

_____

Chapter Wrap-Up

- The effectiveness of the counting method comes from your ability to administer it correctly.

- Remember to explain to your children—when necessary—and then keep quiet. If you have to count, remember to do it calmly, with no emotion in your voice. You'll be amazed when your kids begin to listen!

12
More Serious Offenses in Tweens

Chapter Overview

Sometimes tweens do things that are just too serious for a simple time-out. They may lie, steal, bully, stay out late, smoke or be late to school. Some of these behaviors can become habitual. You need to react in a strong way, but at the same time, you don't want to engage in a battle each time an incident occurs. That isn't good for anyone. This chapter will provide a plan for these especially difficult times. Many parents may never need the Major/Minor System, but it's here in case you do.

Questions About Chapter 12

1. What is the difference between Oppositional Defiant Disorder and Conduct Disorder?

2. Conduct Disorder is the more modern phrase for what expression from the past?

3. Describe the two kinds of lies.

4. Give an example of a minor offense.

5. Give an example of a major offense.

Case Study

Your fifteen-year-old daughter has a weeknight curfew of 10 p.m. She has been pushing this boundary further and further within the last month, so you set up a Major/Minor list of offenses and consequences for your family to follow. On Wednesday evening, she goes out with a group of friends and is reminded once again that her curfew is 10 p.m. She responds rudely, saying, "I know!!" and walks out the door. Ten o'clock comes and goes. Not only isn't she home, but you can't reach her either. She finally rolls in a little after 1 a.m.

What Would You Suggest?

1. Would you consider this a minor, medium or major offense?

    _____

2. What is one of the most important things that you, as the parent, need to remember right when she enters the house?

    _____

    _____

How Are Things at Your House?

1. Think of your children one at a time. Is there one (or more than one) of your children for whom having a Major/Minor System in place would be helpful?

    _____

    _____

    _____

2. Have any of your children already engaged in any of these more serious offenses? If so, which offenses?

_____

_____

_____

Putting *1-2-3 Magic* Into Action with Your Family

1. Without looking at the chapter again (for now), create a list of what you would consider **major offenses** in your household.

_____

_____

_____

_____

2. Now, again without looking at the chapter, create a list of what you would consider **major consequences**.

_____

_____

_____

_____

3. Go back and look at the chapter. How do your lists match up with the lists in Chapter 12? Are they more or less severe? How do you feel about this?

_____

_____

Troubleshooting Exercises

If your child engages in what you would consider a major offense for the first time, your own embarrassment and shock can throw you into a tailspin. Remember how important it is to listen first and respond with a consequence afterwards. Think about exactly what you might initially say to your child after a first major offense. Thinking this through now will help you if you ever find yourself in this emotionally charged situation.

Remember that Oppositional Defiant Disorder can become the much more toxic Conduct Disorder if not handled early. What are the ways in which ODD should be dealt with according to Chapter 12?

_____

_____

Chapter Wrap-Up

■ One good reason for using *1-2-3 Magic* is to prevent the development of Oppositional Defiant Disorder and, even more importantly, Conduct Disorder.

■ When using the Major/Minor System for more serious problems, remember to keep your negative emotions in check!

CAUTION
When using the Major/Minor System, make sure the consequences aren't so harsh that they backfire. And build in some kind of reward for a child's going a number of days or weeks without any problem at all. That's an accomplishment that should be recognized!

13
Establishing Positive Routines

Chapter Overview

After getting a handle on Stop behavior, now it is time to tackle Start behavior. Start behaviors are those things you want your children to start doing, like cleaning their rooms and completing homework. In this chapter you will learn how to train your children by helping them master routines. You will find out how to define and rehearse procedures to establish routines, and you will discover seven Start behavior tactics to use in your training. Remember to keep in mind one of the basic rules of *1-2-3 Magic:* Train the children or keep quiet!

Questions About Chapter 13

1. What are the first two steps to establishing routines?
2. What are three problems that can occur with requests?
3. What is the basic concept of The Docking System?
4. What are a few situations where Natural Consequences might be appropriate?
5. When should you use artificial reinforcers?

Case Study

Brenda has been struggling with her strong-willed son Josiah. He's tough to wake up in the morning and he's even worse to get to bed at night. Josiah is in the third grade and now Brenda has to get him to do his homework. Brenda has tried counting Josiah. The counting does make some impact, but the effect on homework doesn't last very long. Brenda often resorts to yelling, but she then feels very guilty afterwards.

What Would You Suggest?

1. What would you tell Brenda about her use of counting in these situations?

_____

_____

_____

2. What are some tactics that might help Josiah get into a good morning and bedtime routine?

_____

_____

_____

Quik Tip

With Start behavior, you can use more than one tactic at a time for a particular problem. You may even come up with some of your own strategies. Remember: Train the kids to do what you want, or keep quiet!

How Are Things at Your House?

On scale of 1 to 5 (with 1 being TERRIBLE and 5 being PERFECT), how are you doing motivating your children in the Start behavior category?

TERRIBLE				PERFECT
1	2	3	4	5

What is your biggest Start behavior problem? How are you trying to manage it?

_____

_____

Putting *1-2-3 Magic* Into Action with Your Family

Once you've mastered the 1-2-3 counting procedure, it's time to turn your attention to training your kids in Start behavior. Look back at Chapter 2 and look at your list of Start behaviors. What are some of the tactics that might be useful for each of the areas you listed?

START BEHAVIOR	POSSIBLE TACTIC
_____	_____
_____	_____
_____	_____
_____	_____
_____	_____

Troubleshooting Exercise

Anytime you are training your kids for a Start behavior you can expect some testing and manipulation. What kinds of testing do you expect and how will you handle it when your kids try to get you off-track?

_____

_____

_____

Chapter Wrap-Up

- Start behavior requires more motivation from children than Stop behavior
- Use counting first for a week to ten days before tackling Start behavior.
- Be creative with Start behavior.
- Train the kids to do what you want, or keep quiet!

Your 7 Start Behavior Tactics

1. Praise (Positive Reinforcement)
2. Simple Requests
3. Kitchen Timers
4. The Docking System
5. Natural Consequences
6. Charting
7. Counting Variation

Keep your thinking cap on—and good luck!

14
Up and Out in the Morning

Chapter Overview

Getting kids up in the morning can be quite a chore. Many people—both parents and kids—are naturally crabby when they wake up. Combine this crabbiness with the extra pressure of having to be somewhere on time and you have a recipe for disaster. In this chapter you will learn how to use several tactics to train your children to get up and out in the morning. Hang in there! Your mornings could be better in just a few days.

Questions About Chapter 14

1. What does this chapter suggest you do before you design your morning routine?

2. What can you expect from younger children in the mornings?

3. What tactics can you use to help train four- and five-year-olds for getting up and going in the mornings?

4. When can you use counting in the mornings?

5. How do you train older kids to take responsibility for getting up?

Case Study

Rena is having a tough time getting her two kids, ages ten and five, up and out in the morning. Currently she is using the wake-'em-up-and-fuss-at-them-until-they-are-ready plan. Rena desperately would like more peace and more cooperation in the mornings. The more she gets upset with her children the worse they seem to do. She's tried counting and it doesn't seem to do the job. This daily morning chaos makes it hard for Rena to concentrate at work. Her recent performance review was merely satisfactory.

What Would You Suggest?

1. What would you tell Rena about her use of counting in this situation?

_____

_____

2. What tactics could you use to train the younger child? What tactic would be most appropriate for the older child?

_____

_____

_____

_____

Quik Tip

Tell your older kids that from now on, getting up and out in the morning is going to be their responsibility—totally. You will neither supervise nor nag them. Your children will not at first believe you are serious, but they *will* believe you are serious after you've let them get burned a few times. What's your chief job in all this? It's keeping quiet.

How Are Things at Your House?

What plan are you currently using to get your kids up and out in the mornings?

_____

_____

On scale of 1 to 5 (with 1 being TERRIBLE and 5 being PERFECT), how would you rate your attempts at getting your kids up and out in the morning?

TERRIBLE				PERFECT
1	**2**	**3**	**4**	**5**

Putting *1-2-3 Magic* Into Action with Your Family

If getting your kids going in the morning is a problem, outline a plan of action based on this chapter to train your kids for a better morning routine.

_____

_____

Do you have a good morning routine for getting *yourself* going? What is it?

_____

_____

_____

Troubleshooting Exercise

Natural consequences can be very effective but difficult to implement. If you are considering using this technique, take a few minutes and think through the different factors that may come up. Also, think about the manipulation you might encounter. List the ways you plan to handle the kids' testing tactics.

_____

_____

_____

_____

Chapter Wrap-Up

- Preschoolers will need lots of help and praise.

- Young children respond well to praise, charting and timers.

- Older children benefit from natural consequences, but don't expect it to be fun!

15
Cleaning Up and Chores

Chapter Overview

Kids' messiness drives many parents crazy. Their children's rooms are in disarray, their shoes and toys are all over the house, and the kids never seem to do their simple chores. Parents need to remember that cleaning rooms and picking up do not come naturally to kids. Children must be trained to accomplish these tasks. In this chapter you will learn some great principles to help get rooms cleaned, the house picked up and chores completed. And best of all, no nagging, yelling or parental outbursts are required!

Questions About Chapter 15

1. Does counting work to get kids to clean up their rooms?

2. Which room-cleaning option do you like most? Why?

3. What tactics are suggested for getting things picked up?

4. What should be done to encourage younger children to complete their chores?

5. What is the best advice in regard to owning a pet?

Case Study

Allison is fed up with the state of her house. She has three children who are five, nine, and eleven. The kids' rooms are a wreck, toys are all over the house and the dog would starve if Allison relied on the kids' promises to feed the animal. She is tired of reminding, nagging and fussing. She and her husband have met and decided things need to change. The problem is Allison is not sure what to do.

What Do You Suggest?

1. How would you counsel Allison in this situation?

_____

_____

2. What tactics would you begin with to get the children into a routine of cleaning their rooms and completing their chores?

_____

_____

_____

Key Concept

Your kids do not have a right to mess up your entire house! Tell the children that by a certain time every day, anything of theirs that you find lying around will be confiscated and unavailable to them until a certain time the following day. Pick up the kids' things without grumbling or lecturing. You'll soon find that before the magic hour comes each day, the youngsters will be scurrying around to salvage their possessions.

How Are Things at Your House?

On scale of 1 to 5 (with 1 being TERRIBLE and 5 being PERFECT), how would you rate your attempts at getting your children to clean their rooms and complete their chores?

TERRIBLE				PERFECT
1	**2**	**3**	**4**	**5**

What area do you want to focus on first?

_____

_____

_____

Putting *1-2-3 Magic* Into Action with Your Family

1. In the area that you want to begin with, what tactics will you use to train your children?

_____

_____

_____

_____

2. How and when will you begin this process?

_____

_____

_____

Troubleshooting Exercise

Some parents have very high expectations when it comes to keeping things neat and organized. Remember that cleaning, chores and picking up are learned behaviors. So give yourself and your kids a break. Develop a plan, allow some time for your kids to get into the routine, and be sure to praise their accomplishments.

_____

_____

_____

Chapter Wrap-Up

- Children must be trained to clean up their rooms, pick-up and do chores.
- Close the Door, The Weekly Clean-up and Daily Charting are good strategies for cleaning rooms.
- The Kitchen Timer, The Docking System and The Garbage Bag Method work well for picking up.
- Praise, Family Meetings, Charting and The Docking System are good strategies for chores.

16
Suppertime

Chapter Overview

Dinnertime is supposed to be good family time. It's a chance for family members to talk about their day and just enjoy being together. However, with picky eaters, sibling rivalry and tired parents, it can turn into a culinary catastrophe. In this chapter you will learn how to encourage your picky eaters and bring a more relaxed atmosphere to your mealtimes. With just a little planning, eating supper can be a pleasant experience. Indigestion is not fun, but good food should be!

Questions About Chapter 16

1. When is it appropriate to count at the dinner table?

2. What is the basic of idea of using a kitchen timer to get kids into an eating routine?

3. If you use a kitchen timer, what happens to the food when the timer rings?

4. What is the 3-out-of-4 rule?

5. How can you use the Divide-and-Conquer routine to occasionally improve mealtimes?

Case Study

Bill dreads coming home for dinner. Bill and Brenda's youngest son, Joey, has become a handful at the table. Brenda spends most of the mealtime fussing at Joey and trying to get him to eat. Bill then fusses at Brenda for fussing at Joey. Bill and Brenda's oldest son eats quickly and leaves to avoid the conflict. This routine can go on for as much as an hour. The parents have tried letting Joey not eat supper, but then bedtime becomes whining time for sure.

Quik Tip
Try this with your finicky eaters. Give the kids super-small portions and then set the timer for twenty minutes. If the children finish before the timer goes off, they get their dessert. You may not nag or prompt—the timer will do that for you.

What Would You Suggest?

1. Based on this chapter, what could Bill and Brenda do to better manage their picky eater?

   _____

   _____

2. What ideas could they try that would make mealtimes better for their older son?

   _____

   _____

Key Concept
Who says you have to eat dinner together every single night of the year? Consider having some special nights where each person eats wherever she wishes. Or—better yet—have some nights where one parent takes one child out to eat. It's different and it's fun!

How Are Things at Your House?

On scale of 1 to 5 (1 being TERRIBLE and 5 being PERFECT), how would you rate your mealtimes?

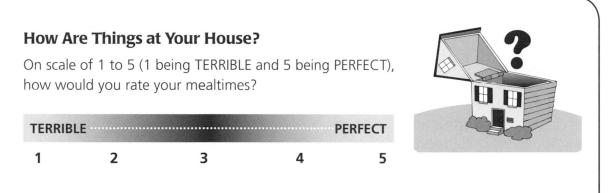

TERRIBLE				PERFECT
1	2	3	4	5

If your mealtimes are not rated as a 5, which tactics do you think would work best for your family?

_____

_____

Putting *1-2-3 Magic* Into Action with Your Family

If you have more then one child and your mealtimes have been chaotic, would you consider the Divide-and-Conquer idea occasionally? If so, when and how will you implement this strategy?

_____

_____

_____

How would *your* kids feel about the Divide-and-Conquer notion?

_____

_____

Troubleshooting Exercise

Many parents forget the No-Talking and No-Emotion rules when it comes to mealtimes. Which ever tactic you choose, remember not to nag or prompt. Allow the strategies to do the work. And remember, relax. No child we know of has died of starvation when good food was available.

How was suppertime managed by your parents? Can any of their ideas help you?

_____

_____

_____

Chapter Wrap-Up

For Picky Eaters try:

- Small Portions and a Kitchen Timer
- The 3-out-of-4 Rule

For more peace at mealtimes occasionally try:

- The Divide-and-Conquer routine
- Not talking

17

Homework

Chapter Overview

Homework civil wars can make school nights miserable for the whole family. Everyone starts dreading after-school and evening times. Though there are no easy answers, there are ways of making homework time more tolerable and productive. In this chapter you will learn about some of these methods, including why routine is critical and how Natural Consequences can sometimes do the trick. You will also discover several other strategies that can help make schoolwork times more bearable for you and your children. Homework is a permanent and necessary evil. Start getting control of it today!

Questions About Chapter 17

1. How can routine cut down on homework issues?
2. How can Natural Consequences help with schoolwork struggles?
3. What is the main rule with the PNP Method?
4. What is the Magic Point in charting for homework?
5. What is the Rough Checkout?

Case Study

Dan and Judy's son, Justin, has struggled with homework for years. Judy tries to help Justin each evening, but she usually comes away frustrated. Justin often forgets his homework assignments and often starts those assignments late in the evening when he does have them. Dan is usually the heavy, but is tired of arguing with Justin. Lately, Mom and Dad have tried staying out of it, but Justin's grades have plummeted. Dan and Judy are frustrated and are not sure what to do.

What Would You Suggest?

1. What would be your first suggestion to Dan and Judy?

_____

_____

_____

2. Would charting be useful in this situation? Why?

_____

_____

_____

_____

_____

Quik Tip

The first thing out of your mouth when your child shows you her homework must be something positive—even if it's just that she brought her work to you. And remember: 8 p.m. is no time for academic perfection!

How Are Things at Your House?

On scale of 1 to 5 (1 being TERRIBLE and 5 being PERFECT), how would you rate your homework and practice routines?

TERRIBLE				PERFECT
1	2	3	4	5

What is the most difficult part of homework time in your house?

_____

_____

Putting *1-2-3 Magic* Into Action with Your Family

1. If your homework routine is not rated as a 5, which tactics do you think would work best for your child?

_____

_____

2. How will you implement these new tactics?

_____

_____

_____

Troubleshooting Exercise

With chronic problems, you will need to take a closer look at why your child is having such a hard time. You may need to set up a time with your child's teacher or counselor to discuss a possible learning disability or other impairment. Don't wait! The sooner you diagnose a problem, the sooner you can help your child.

Chapter Wrap-Up

- Routine is critical.
- Develop a strategy and stick with it.
- Try to get homework done before dinner.
- You can also use homework strategies for practicing obnoxious musical instruments.

Homework Helpers

1. No spontaneous requests!
2. Natural consequences
3. The Positive-Negative-Positive (PNP) Method
4. The Rough Checkout
5. Charting

18
Going to Bed—And Staying There!

Chapter Overview

Putting kids to bed and keeping them there can be a daily nightmare for many frazzled parents. Often a parent and child can get locked into a battle that ends with arguing and screaming. Then no one feels like sleeping! However, there is a better way. In this chapter you will learn about The Basic Bedtime Method that can actually make bedtime an enjoyable experience. You will also find some tips on how to handle kids getting out of bed and the inevitable nighttime waking that most kids go through.

Questions About Chapter 17

1. What is the first thing you must do in The Basic Bedtime Method?

2. If you are having trouble coming up with all the things that need to be done to get ready for bed, what does the book suggest?

3. What are the purposes of the special time before bed?

4. How do you handle a child getting out of bed?

5. What are the basic steps to handle nighttime waking?

Case Study

Christy has a terrible time with her son Ben most evenings. Her struggle begins with homework and continues through trying to get him to go to bed each night. Lately, she has offered Ben the option of later bedtimes if he finishes his homework. The trouble is that no bedtime is late enough. He still wants to stay up later. Christy is very frustrated and doesn't know what to do.

What Would You Suggest?

1. Do you think changing the bedtime is a good idea?

_____

_____

_____

2. What would you suggest to Christy for getting Ben to bed?

_____

_____

_____

CAUTION

Never forget one very important fact: If a child won't stay in bed at bedtime, the longer he is up and the farther away he gets from his bedroom, the more reinforcement he will get from that activity. Your job? Cut him off at the pass.

How Are Things at Your House?

On a scale of 1 to 5, how would you rate your current bedtime ritual (1 means it is TERRIBLE and 5 means that it is GREAT)?

TERRIBLE				GREAT
1	**2**	**3**	**4**	**5**

Do you have any problems keeping your child in the bed after bedtime or during the night? Explain.

_____

_____

_____

Putting *1-2-3 Magic* Into Action with Your Family

What are some ideas you could implement to improve your family's bedtime plan?

_____

_____

If you have a spouse or partner, how would you use more free time in the evening?

_____

_____

Troubleshooting Exercises

If you have more than one child, bedtime can be even more of a challenge. You may need to stagger bedtimes or alternate certain tasks with your spouse. Write your plans here.

_____

_____

_____

What are the bedtimes you will pick for each of your kids?

_____

_____

_____

Chapter Wrap-Up

- Set a bedtime and stick to it.
- Use The Basic Bedtime Method to get kids to bed.
- The longer a child stays up, the more reinforcement he gets.
- No lights or talking during nighttime waking

19
Sympathetic Listening

Chapter Overview

Your children will sometimes surprise you with their comments. Your daughter, for example, screams, "I hate school! The work is too hard!" Your immediate reaction may be to scream right back, "Hey! Don't yell at me! That's 1!" Think about this for a minute, though. Your daughter is clearly frustrated and angry. Is she screaming *at* you or is she screaming *to* you? There is a definite difference. While screaming may not be the best way to deal with her frustration, keep in mind, she's a kid! Most kids don't know how to effectively express their negative emotions. Right now, your daughter needs a sympathetic listener and not a disciplinarian.

Questions About Chapter 19

1. List the three steps to sympathetic listening.

2. What two things does sympathetic listening try to accomplish?

3. Explain the phrase, "Anxious parent, angry child."

4. Why does consistent and pointless repetition of worries by the parent aggravate kids?

5. How should you decide when to listen and when to count?

Case Study

Dan's daughter, Tina, has been outside playing with friends. Dan has just gotten home from work and is finally beginning to relax a bit when he starts to hear voices raised outside. Suddenly Tina runs in the front door and slams it shut. She screams, "I HATE Jenny! She's always trying to take my friends away from me!"

Tina knows not to slam the door and Dan definitely doesn't appreciate her screaming at him. He's tired from work, which makes his annoyance even more pronounced. He looks at her sternly and says, "That's 1."

What Would You Do?

1. In the same situation, what would you have said to Tina instead of "That's 1"?

    _____

    _____

2. How likely is it that Tina will continue to come to her father with her problems in the future?

    _____

    _____

CAUTION

1. You are a **good listener** if, while your child is talking, you are sincerely trying to understand what he is saying.

2. You are a **bad listener** if, while your child is talking, you are preparing your rebuttal.

How Are Things at Your House?

1. Do you think you are generally a sympathetic listener?

_____

2. Can you think of a circumstance when you have
responded to one of your children the way Dan did to Tina? If so,
describe the situation.

_____

_____

Putting *1-2-3 Magic* Into Action with Your Family

Do you tend to worry unnecessarily? Does your spouse/parenting partner tend
to do this as well?

_____

_____

List three things that you can tell yourself when you begin to worry too much that
can help you to "backpedal," see the bigger picture and avoid overparenting.

_____

_____

_____

Troubleshooting Exercises

Keep in mind that the older your kids get, the more you are going to want them to come to you with their problems. Their problems only become bigger and much more serious as they enter their teen years. You want your children to know from a young age that you are a safe place for them to come to when they are troubled.

It can be difficult to remember that it is our job as parents to help our kids to become self sufficient, independent thinkers. We have them for a short time so that we can teach them what they need to know in order to move on and become productive, happy adults. Trying to stay aware of this will help you fight off the urge to overparent your children.

Chapter Wrap-Up

- We **listen** to problems and we **count** attacks. It's important to recognize the difference.

- You don't want your children to feel that they will get yelled at every time they try to discuss unpleasant situations or feelings, even if they aren't handling their emotions exactly as you would like them to.

Overparenting is the opposite of listening!

20
Real Magic: One-on-One Fun

Chapter Overview

Having fun with another human being is at the center of all relationships. In fact, any relationship that we *choose* to enter into (friendship, romance) usually begins because we find that we have fun with that other person! Having fun with your child—just the two of you—can be magical. It's one of the most important things you can do for your relationship. When you seek your child out to say, "Hey, let's play a game!" what your child hears is, "Hey, I like you and I think you're really cool to hang out with!" He feels valued and special. There is no greater gift that you can give to your child.

Questions About Chapter 20

1. Why is having fun with your child important for a positive relationship with her?

2. What are two reasons why family fun can be difficult?

3. Why is it important to find time for one-on-one fun, as opposed to always having family fun?

4. Why is it important to find an activity that *both you and your child* enjoy doing?

5. What are some examples of simple, inexpensive one-on-one fun?

Case Study

Susan's eight-year-old son, Trevor, walks into the kitchen complaining that he's bored. It's almost the end of summer and most of the "free time" activities that he usually engages in are getting stale and boring—except for one! Trevor loves to play with his Star Wars action figures anywhere, anytime. Susan suggests to Trevor that he go play with those, but he responds that it's no fun alone and none of his friends are home. "Will you play with me, Mom?"

If there is one thing that Susan detests, it's playing with Star Wars action figures. She has no idea how to "pretend" the way she's supposed to, and it always ends up with Trevor getting frustrated with her for "not doing it right." On the other hand, she hasn't spent any one-on-one fun time with him lately and she supposes that this could fill the bill. She goes to play with him, but, as predicted, she does it "wrong" and he ends up getting annoyed with her. She's happy to be finished with it—she hates that game anyway!

What Would You Do?

1. Does the activity above count as one-on-one shared fun?

_____

2. What should Susan do about the problem?

_____

_____

_____

Quik Tip

To like your kids you must enjoy them regularly. And for them to respond well to your discipline, they must enjoy and like you too. That means only one thing: You'd better find regular time to play with your youngsters!

How Are Things at Your House?

Think of your children one at a time. On a scale of 1 to 5 (1 being NOT OFTEN AT ALL and 5 being VERY OFTEN), assign a number to each child according to how often the two of you have one-on-one fun on a regular basis.

NOT OFTEN	···	VERY OFTEN

1	2	3	4	5

_____

If it seems one of your children is getting "less" of you or conversely, that one of your children is getting "more" of you, think about why that may be. What can you do to even things up?

_____

_____

Putting *1-2-3 Magic* Into Action with Your Family

Write lists of five things (one list for each of your children) that you could do to have fun together. Remember that what is fun for one of your children may not be fun for another!

CHILD:	CHILD:	CHILD:
1. _____	1. _____	1. _____
2. _____	2. _____	2. _____
3. _____	3. _____	3. _____
4. _____	4. _____	4. _____
5. _____	5. _____	5. _____

When you look at your family's lifestyle and schedule, how often do you think you can manage to spend thirty minutes of uninterrupted fun time with each of your children? Daily? Weekly? Monthly? Is this often enough? Do you need to reprioritize a bit?

_____

_____

Troubleshooting Exercises

1. Sometimes your relationship with your child is a bit rocky. It can be difficult to have "shared fun" with someone you argue with anytime either of you opens your mouth! However, this is the child who probably needs the time with you most of all. Name an activity that can be fun but that really requires minimal interaction (or opportunity for conflict).

_____

_____

2. Sometimes, money can be an issue. Remember that shared fun can be something as simple and inexpensive as catching fireflies together. One-on-one fun doesn't have to cost you a dime! List some fun and inexpensive activities.

_____

_____

_____

_____

Chapter Wrap-Up

Any two people who make the time to regularly have fun together will have a healthy rapport. It's one of the most important things that you can do for your relationship with your child!

21
When Can You Talk?

Chapter Overview

Does *1-2-3 Magic* insist that you don't talk to your children? No! There is a place for talking to your children in order to teach them the values that you want to impart. The problems arise when you talk to them when you're angry and frustrated and you talk so much that they aren't even hearing you anymore! Calm, rational, concise conversations, when you and your child are not experiencing the "heat of battle" are the best means of providing your child with the information you want her to have. Chapter 21 shows you how to talk to your children most effectively.

Questions About Chapter 21

1. What are the four sets of skills your children need to possess in order to have good, satisfying lives?

2. What are the three ways your children are going to learn these skills?

3. What is meant by the term "behavioral rehearsal"?

4. What are a few forms of talking that you need to avoid when speaking to your children?

5. When is it a bad time to talk to your child?

Case Study

Cindy's five-year-old son, Max, has grabbed a toy from his brother for the fourth time today. Max is bigger than his younger brother, can easily overpower him and does it often. Frankly, Cindy is concerned that Max is becoming a little bully!

Max grabs the truck from his brother again and Cindy has had enough. It's time that they have a serious talk about how to treat others! Cindy grabs the truck right back from Max and gives it back to his brother. Max immediately begins to scream. Cindy tells him that he is behaving very badly and that she is disappointed in him. She says, "It doesn't feel so nice when someone grabs something from you, does it?" She has to scream to be heard over Max's yelling, which is getting louder with every passing minute.

What Would You Suggest?

1. Do you see a problem with how Cindy has handled this situation?
If so, what?

_____

_____

2. Given what you have learned in this chapter, explain how you would handle this same episode.

_____

_____

_____

How Are Things at Your House?

Think of your children one at a time. On a scale of 1 to 5 (1 being NOT LIKELY and 5 being VERY LIKELY), assign a number to each child according to how likely you are to get into **frequent arguments** with them.

NOT LIKELY		....		VERY LIKELY
1	2	3	4	5

Rate each of your children individually.

Child: _____ **Rate:** _____

Child: _____ **Rate:** _____

Child: _____ **Rate:** _____

Child: _____ **Rate:** _____

Which child received the highest score? What can you do to avoid these situations with him or her in the future?

_____

_____

_____

_____

_____

Quik Tip

Don't ever underestimate how much *behavioral rehearsal* is required before kids can master skills such as using a fork, not biting other kids, talking in a normal voice when frustrated, organizing homework, remembering to pick up after themselves, and making and keeping friends.

Putting *1-2-3 Magic* Into Action with Your Family

1. Can you think of any behavior in which you currently engage that you wouldn't want your child to imitate? If so, can you make the necessary changes to ensure that they don't? What would those changes be?

_____

_____

2. Make a list of the people who are currently in your child's life whose influence you will need to monitor.

_____

_____

_____

Troubleshooting Exercise

Many children are very good at baiting us into talking to them during times when we are already angry or frustrated with their behavior. This is called arguing! Think of a few ways to avoid being led down this path by your child.

_____

_____

Chapter Wrap-Up

There is definitely a place for talking when teaching children. However, the time for talking is not when you are angry or in the moment when your child's negative behavior requires a consequence. That's the time for action, not words.

22
Solving Problems Together

Chapter Overview

Wouldn't it be nice if we could all live peacefully together all of the time? Too bad life doesn't work that way! With busy schedules, financial pressures, sibling rivalry and a whole host of other dynamics, peace is sometimes hard to maintain in a family. One way to facilitate peace and foster much more independence in your children is to have regular family meetings. These sometimes not-so-much-fun meetings can solve many of a family's daily problems. In this chapter, you will learn how to run a family meeting and how to address the big and small issues that regularly come up in your family.

Questions About Chapter 21

1. What does it mean to move from a benevolent dictatorship to an "almost but not quite" democracy?

2. When should you start family meetings?

3. Why should you have family meetings?

4. What are the basic steps to a family meeting?

5. Do you ever have a one-on-one meeting with a child to try to solve a problem?

Case Study

Casey tried a family meeting, but it did not go well. Her three-year-old child kept interrupting and her nine-year-old twin girls just argued with one another. Casey wanted to involve her children in some family decisions, but they just didn't seem to be interested. Casey finally counted the girls and sent them to their rooms. She really would like to use family meetings, but she thinks they won't work for her family.

What Would You Suggest?

1. What problems do you see in the case study that might have contributed to the failed meeting?

_____

_____

2. What guidelines could Casey implement that might help a family meeting work for her?

_____

_____

_____

_____

Quik Tip

Many parents agree that the family meeting is one of the most *aggravating* and one of the most *effective* things you can do with your children. Don't ever expect anyone to want to come!

How Are Things at Your House?

1. What are some specific issues that your family could address in a family meeting?

    _____

    _____

    _____

2. How do you think your children will respond to a family meeting?

    _____

    _____

Putting *1-2-3 Magic* Into Action with Your Family

When would be a good time for you to call a family meeting?

Day: _____   Time: _____

Write a simple plan for your first family meeting.

_____

_____

_____

_____

_____

Troubleshooting Exercises

Family meetings can easily break down if you are not careful. One thing to watch out for is one child becoming the scapegoat. Be careful to keep the meeting focused on the issues and not on a particular person.

Pay attention to your own tolerance for family meetings. Can you go over an hour and remain patient and calm?

Chapter Wrap-Up

- ■ Keep family meetings short and focused. You'll find they are a useful tool in teaching your children valuable life skills!

- ■ Use a one-on-one meeting when you want to discuss an issue privately with one of your youngsters.

Family meetings and one-on-one meetings are not always fun. But they help prepare your kids for one of life's ultimate challenges...
Living with someone else!

23
Kids, Tweens and Tech

Chapter Overview

Technological communication has exploded in the last few years. It's everywhere and we can't escape it! "Techcom" has some wonderful uses, for sure. Used wisely and in moderation, technological advances can help our kids in many different ways. But how do we manage them? We learn how to introduce these tech devices into our children's lives and then we teach the kids how to use them safely and responsibly. We establish rules for using technology and then monitor our children. We can make sure that our children receive the benefits of technological communication while limiting the risks.

Questions About Chapter 23

1. Who are the three members of the "triple alliance"?

2. Write down one good thing about techcom in our kids' lives.

3. Write down one bad thing about techcom in our kids' lives.

4. According to Malcolm Gladwell, author of *The Outliers*, how long does a person have to practice a specific skill before becoming a success?

5. Who can bewildered parents use for consultants regarding the techcom world?

Case Study (Prepare for the Future!)

Amanda's daughter, Taylor, is fourteen years old and has always been a good kid. Lately, however, Amanda is seeing less and less of her daughter. It seems she is either at school, with friends or shut up in her bedroom online. She emerges for food and that is about all.

At dinner one evening, Taylor begins talking about her new boyfriend. He's a fifteen-year-old boy she met online. To Amanda's horror, Taylor already met with him in person, all on her own, without ever having said a word about it to her mom or dad. When Amanda asks her why she hadn't asked permission, she said, "Mom, it's no big deal! I meet up with friends that I meet online all the time!" Taylor hadn't met with harm when meeting her online friend, but Amanda still shudders when she thinks about what *could* have happened to her daughter.

What Would You Do?

1. Should Taylor's computer be in her bedroom? Where would you put her computer?

_____

2. If you were Amanda, what would you say to Taylor after having heard the news of her new boyfriend?

_____

_____

_____

_____

Quik Tip

Most Internet filters and cell phone companies have parental controls that allow you to turn off the device during specified times. This can be very helpful to keep kids off the Internet at night and off the phone during school hours.

How Are Things at Your House?

1. What are some specific rules that you think need to be in place for children regarding their technological devices?

_____

_____

_____

2. What are some positive things that you believe technological communication can bring to your family's lives?

_____

_____

Putting *1-2-3 Magic* Into Action with Your Family

1. At what age do you believe your children should have access to the Internet? How about cell phones? Explain.

Internet: _____   Cell phones:_____

_____

2. Where are the computers located in your home? How about the televisions? Do you think that their locations provide too much access to bad information for your children?

_____

_____

Troubleshooting Exercises

1. Allowing your children to keep their computers in their bedrooms is a recipe for trouble. All computers should be kept in a public place, such as a family room or kitchen. If your children want to have private conversations with their friends, they can do that in person. The computer is not the place for them to do that.

2. Online bullying is becoming a bigger and bigger problem with kids, tweens and teens. Make sure to discuss this issue with your child before allowing him to use online tools. Discuss the importance of treating others with respect, as well as the importance of coming forward when he or someone that he knows is experiencing online bullying.

3. What will your guidelines be for screentime hours per day for your children?

_____

_____

Chapter Wrap-Up

Technology is always changing, and our kids are tech savvy! Stay involved, talk to your kids and other parents, and you can keep a handle on your children's techcom lives!

Don't expect yourself to be knowledgeable about every aspect of techcom and techplay. Shop around for a good parent consultant.

How much is the techcom revolution babysitting your kids?

_____

_____

24
Staying on the Wagon

Chapter Overview

Sometimes when things go well in our lives, we forget the times when they weren't going so great. This is especially true of parenting. You're probably going through this workbook now because you are having some rough times. After you have begun tackling your three parenting jobs, though, things are likely to get better pretty quickly. This is great news! But what happens after your life gets a bit easier? You may slip—or "fall off the wagon." There are several reasons this may happen, but there are also some easy ways to get right back on track.

Questions About Chapter 24

1. In *1-2-3 Magic*, what does the term "slipping" mean?
2. List three reasons that slipping can occur over the long term.
3. List three emotional obstacles that may cause slipping.
4. How does one recover from short-term slipping?
5. How does one recover from long-term slipping?

Case Study

Mike and his wife Anne have been successfully using *1-2-3 Magic* for many months. Their lives had gotten so much easier there for a while. In the past weeks, though, Mike has noticed that chaos is beginning to take hold again and it's annoying him. Mike and Anne are not counting as much, but they are talking and yelling more.

One Sunday afternoon Mike is lying on the couch watching football. It's the only relaxation he gets all week, and he needs it! He begins to hear a fight gearing up in one of the kid's rooms. He is furious. All he asks for is a few hours of peace, one day a week! He heads upstairs, screaming the whole way. He'll take care of these kids!

What Would You Suggest?

1. What is the real problem that this family is facing?

_____

_____

2. How should Mike handle this situation?

_____

_____

_____

_____

Quik Tip
When you're doing nine things at once, who can remember the No-Talking and No-Emotion rules? *You can!*

How Are Things at Your House?

1. Which of the emotional obstacles currently give you the most trouble when you're dealing with your children?

_____

_____

2. Write about a specific instance when this particular emotional obstacle has been a problem for you.

_____

_____

_____

Putting *1-2-3 Magic* Into Action with Your Family

Are there any triggers for slipping coming up in your immediate future (such as a new baby, a vacation, visitors, etc.)?

_____

If so, how will you prepare for this event?

_____

_____

_____

Troubleshooting Exercises

Falling off the wagon does not mean *1-2-3 Magic* is not working. It simply means you're not working temporarily. Nobody's perfect!

Just like with anything that you take on in your life, preparation is key in parenting. Think ahead a few months or years. When you slip up in the future, write down how you will catch yourself and how you will handle the setback.

Chapter Wrap-Up

- A certain amount of slipping is normal. You are human! All you have to do when it happens is get back to basics.

- If necessary, redo the Kickoff Conversation.

- Enjoy the recovery!

25
Your New Life

Chapter Overview

You made it to the end! You now understand how to do your three parenting jobs. You're ready to control obnoxious behavior, encourage positive behavior and build strong relationships with each of your children. Your life is about to change! No, your children will not sprout angel wings, but if you do *1-2-3 Magic* correctly, you will find that a lot more peace (and fun!) is going to make its way into all your lives.

Questions About Chapter 25

1. How will *1-2-3 Magic* help to improve your children's self-esteem?

2. How will *1-2-3 Magic* help to improve your self-esteem?

3. Why is parenting so exhausting for so many parents?

4. List the ways in which *1-2-3 Magic* will help you spend more positive time with your kids.

5. Are there any factors in your life that might sabotage your success?

Case Study

Carol's eight-year-old son, Tim, is a constant problem when it comes to doing his homework. He never wants to get started. Carol's next-door neighbor, Susan, can't stand the constant whining of her four-year-old daughter, Meghan. She seems to whine whenever she wants anything! Susan's brother, Mark, just told her over the phone that he is getting the feeling that he and his eleven-year-old son, Matthew, don't seem to enjoy each other's company so much anymore This is starting to worry him a lot as the boy heads to adolescence.

What Would You Suggest?

1. What should Carol do?

_____

2. What should Susan do?

_____

3. What should Mark do?

_____

4. Which parenting job is each of these parents dealing with?

Carol: _____

Susan: _____

Mark: _____

How Are Things at Your House?

1. Which of your children will be the biggest challenge for you in implementing *1-2-3 Magic*?

   _____

   Why? _____

   _____

2. How will you work to manage your own feelings of frustration while helping this child "get with the program"?

   _____

   _____

Putting *1-2-3 Magic* Into Action with Your Family

Why do you think that the first parenting step deals with handling Stop behaviors?

_____

_____

With which parenting step do you think you will have the easiest time? How about the hardest time?

_____

_____

Troubleshooting Exercises

Remember that some slipping is normal! Keep in mind that certain family situations and just plain time can cause this to happen. What are some slipping triggers that you need to watch out for?

Although slipping may mean you're going through a difficult time, it does not mean there's something wrong with you.

Wrap-Up

Explain each diagram.

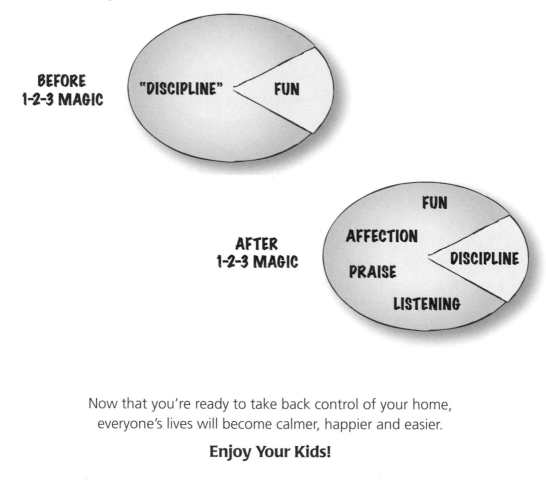

Now that you're ready to take back control of your home,
everyone's lives will become calmer, happier and easier.

Enjoy Your Kids!

Stories and Questions

Counting Obnoxious Behavior

Many parents, when they are starting the *1-2-3 Magic* program, begin by simply counting obnoxious behavior for a few days to a week before they do anything with parenting Jobs #2 and #3, encouraging good behavior and strengthening relationships. That's the way my husband and I handled it and it was a good move!

In **The Case of the Temper Tantrum Terrorist**, you'll meet our young five-year-old son, Zach. Before *1-2-3 Magic* this kid was a handful. While I've heard that many children (about 50%) will shape up in just a few days with counting, it took us about a week to make Zach a "believer."

Here's our story. In the **WRONG WAY** section, you'll see two bewildered parents. Then you'll sit in on our **THINKING IT THROUGH** before we get around to handling our son the **RIGHT WAY**.

TEMPER TANTRUM TERRORIST

APPLE PIE!!

I must admit, I don't like
to think about our life before
1-2-3 Magic. Our home was run by a
five year old. If our son, Zach, didn't get his way, he resorted to
kicking, screaming or crying. We spent so much time making sure
Zach was happy that we remained miserable. Going to the store
required both parents, eating out was an exercise in futility,
and neighborhood barbeques were politely declined.

One night we took a chance and went to a local restaurant...

Well, the first round went to Zach—in a sense. Actually, it didn't go to anybody, since we all wound up feeling miserable. You can't beat public humiliation for pure fun—and, believe me, we'd been through plenty of scenes like the one you just witnessed.

We just couldn't keep on going like this. We were getting discouraged and we had to do something different. But just exactly what was that "something" going to be? Usually the mom is the one to get the ball rolling with problems like this, and our house was no exception.

Feeling desperate, I decided to try a product that I thought at the time would be a long shot.

 After our talk, there were times when I thought my husband was understanding what I was saying, but most of the time I felt I wasn't getting anywhere. He hadn't read the book, so I got the *1-2-3 Magic* DVD (which, I thought, was just as good as the book). My husband hinted—but only hinted—that he might be willing to watch the DVD, but only if I wasn't in the room!

Why are adult males so hard to talk to? Zach's behavior remained awful. As far as I was concerned, we were still in a big pickle— stuck with nowhere to go.

NOWHERE
5 MILES

— Then one day a miracle occurred —

THINKING IT THROUGH

My husband actually watched the *1-2-3 Magic* DVD. And he liked it!

We practiced counting on each other.

THAT'S 2.

We whispered about our plans—Zach's suspicious eyes watched us.

I CAN BEAT THIS.

We had the Kickoff Conversation.

ZACH, WE'RE GOING TO DO SOME THINGS DIFFERENT AROUND HERE.

My husband and I were a team! We were ready for whatever he could throw at us.

123

Since our "week from hell," things have been very different around our house. Our son now knows that when we say something, we mean business. No yelling, no empty threats. Sure, he still pushes the limits at times, but he doesn't get anywhere.

We've also advanced in our use of *1-2-3 Magic* to the strategies for encouraging good behavior (like getting Zach to bed) and to doing things that reinforce the bond between us (like shared fun). Since we have learned how to control Zach's oppositional moments, it is so much easier to like him!

Keep in mind that when you start counting your kids, you may not have to go through a hell week like we did. But honestly, if we started our stories in this book with the tale of a youngster shaping up in just a few hours (it's happened many times!), you wouldn't believe us, would you?

We hope our harrowing tale has given you some encouragement!

Questions & Answers for You

Before they start the *1-2-3 Magic* program, many parents are skeptical about whether or not this new method will work. Moms and dads can still be somewhat hesitant even after reading the book or watching the DVDs.

There are several reasons why parents sometimes feel doubtful before using *1-2-3 Magic*. Let's look at four of these concerns, then we'll ask you a few questions about what is known as the Little Adult Assumption.

CONCERN #1
When frustrated, your child is ferocious!

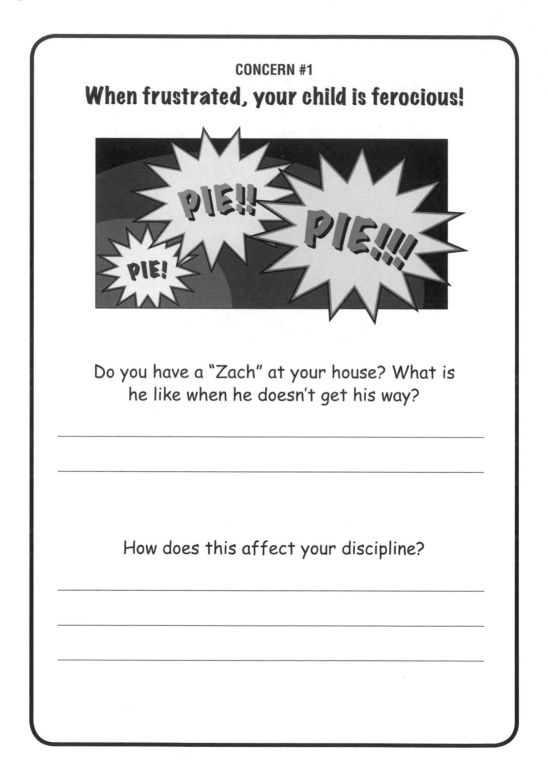

Do you have a "Zach" at your house? What is he like when he doesn't get his way?

_____

_____

How does this affect your discipline?

_____

_____

_____

CONCERN #2

You feel like you've tried everything.

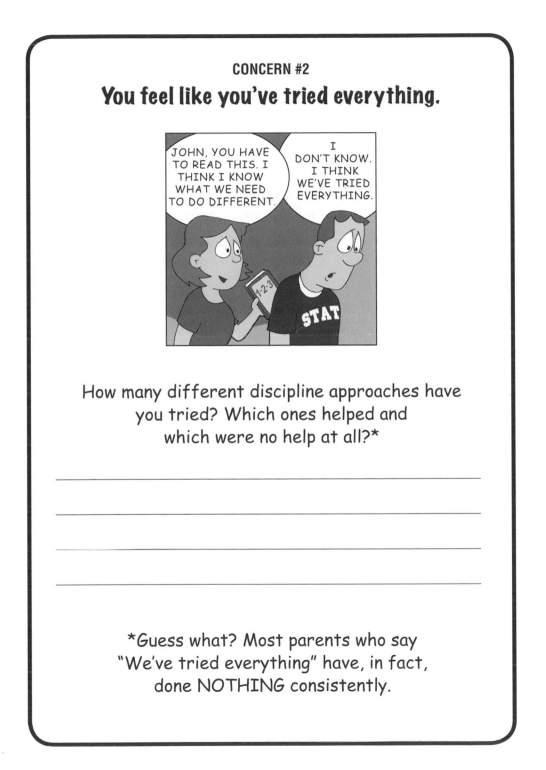

How many different discipline approaches have you tried? Which ones helped and which were no help at all?*

_____

_____

_____

_____

*Guess what? Most parents who say "We've tried everything" have, in fact, done NOTHING consistently.

CONCERN #3
Counting seems too simple or too wimpy.

What was your first reaction to
Mom's strategy in the scene above?

_____

_____

What was Zach's first reaction? What was his
reaction to the 2nd and 3rd counts?

_____

_____

_____

CONCERN #4

We should be able to talk everything over with our kids.

Do you think Zach's father had a feeling of impending doom at this point?

_____

_____

When your children are frustrated, how often do your explanations resolve the problem?

_____

_____

Other Questions ...

What would you think if Zach had reacted like this to his parents' comments?

_____

_____

_____

Other Questions ...

What is happening to Zach's ANGER LEVEL as the "conversation" continues?

_____

How will this affect the chances of his cooperating?

_____

Think about this ...

WE HAD AN ODD SITUATION
WITH ZACH WHERE

MORE TALKING
produced
LESS COOPERATION

If talking sometimes makes matters worse in a crisis,
why do we parents continue to do it?

_____

_____

_____

And finally ...

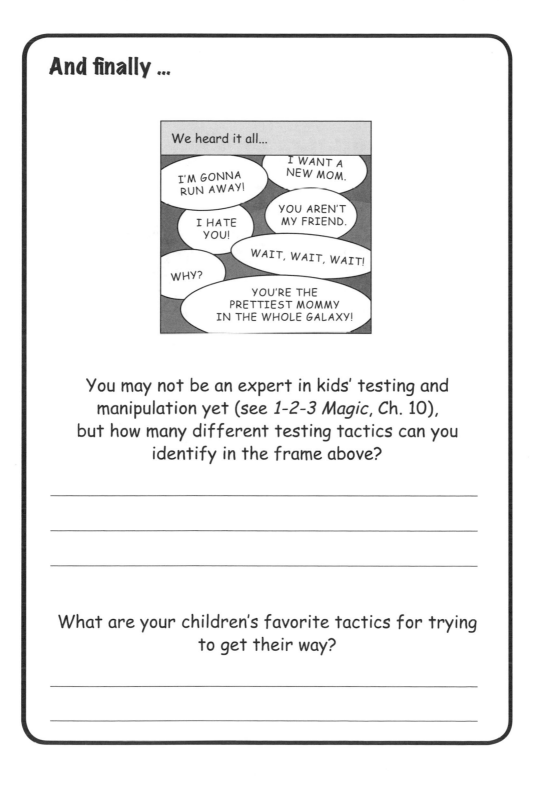

We heard it all...

I'M GONNA RUN AWAY!

I WANT A NEW MOM.

I HATE YOU!

YOU AREN'T MY FRIEND.

WAIT, WAIT, WAIT!

WHY?

YOU'RE THE PRETTIEST MOMMY IN THE WHOLE GALAXY!

You may not be an expert in kids' testing and manipulation yet (see *1-2-3 Magic*, Ch. 10), but how many different testing tactics can you identify in the frame above?

_____

_____

_____

What are your children's favorite tactics for trying to get their way?

_____

_____

Sibling Rivalry

Parenting is a difficult and complicated job. Admit it now, it's a lot harder than you ever imagined it would be before you had kids! Once our little ones showed up in our house, there they were—period. No escape and no going out without a babysitter.

Before we had children, my husband and I imagined the warm, fuzzy, peaceful and affectionate times we would have with our youngsters. But after several years of parenting experience, we quickly learned that we also had to manage whining, teasing, tantrums, messiness and not wanting to go to bed.

We also found out that two kids is a lot harder than one. Sibling rivalry is chronic and it's one of the most aggravating things kids can do. Managing and minimizing kids' fighting is part of Parenting Job #1.

Check out this story ...

One day, on our way home from the grocery store, my children were passing the time looking for pictures in the clouds. This is a favorite game of theirs, and I love hearing their creative ideas. On this particular day my six-year-old daughter suddenly said...

THE INCREDIBLE CASE OF THE

TRAVELING TROUBLEMAKERS

Questions for You

On a scale from 1 to 5, how aggravating would this scene be for you?

VERY AGGRAVATING

1   2   3   4   5

List three things this mother would like to say
(but should not say!) at this point:

1. _____

2. _____

3. _____

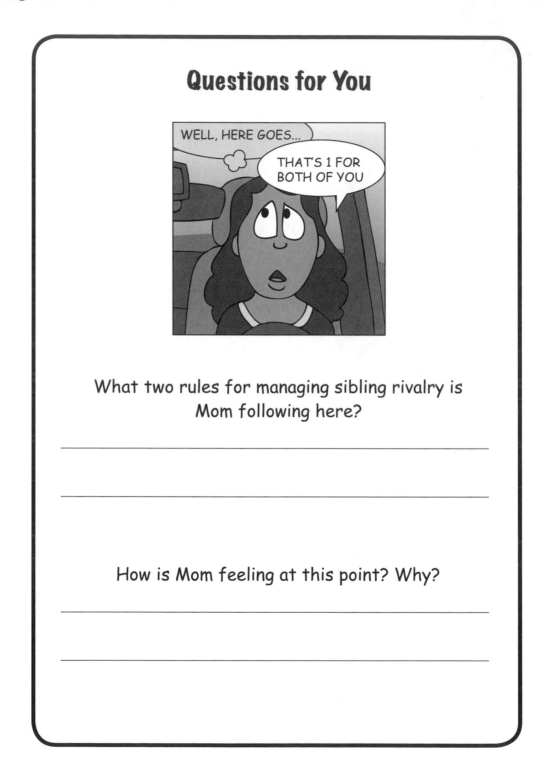

Questions for You

What two rules for managing sibling rivalry is Mom following here?

_____

_____

_____

How is Mom feeling at this point? Why?

_____

_____

Questions for You

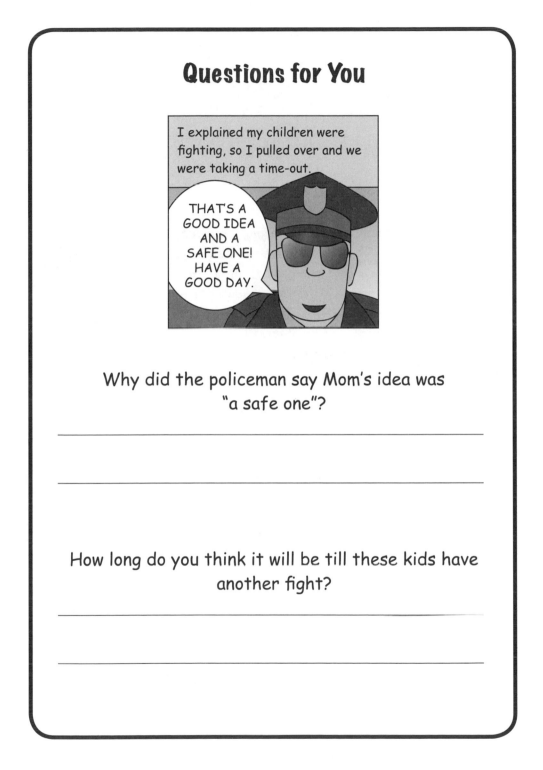

Why did the policeman say Mom's idea was "a safe one"?

_____

_____

How long do you think it will be till these kids have another fight?

_____

_____

Encouraging Positive Routines

As you have learned from *1-2-3 Magic*, a big part of Parenting Job #2, Encouraging Good Behavior, is establishing reasonable and consistent routines. Kids do much better when the things you want them to accomplish, like eating supper and homework, are carried out each day at the same time and pretty much in the same way.

One of the most critical daily routines is getting the kids to bed— and getting them to stay there. Mess this job up and everyone will pay dearly, not only in the evening but the next day as well. That's what happened to us. We had to learn the hard way how to do bedtime with our young daughter, but what a relief once we figured it out!

Here's our story ...

Obviously, this nighttime routine was one that we couldn't keep up for much longer. The funny thing was that we already had the *1-2-3 Magic* book, and we had been successfully using counting during the day with our daughter. But we didn't see how in the world counting would help us with our little girl's refusing to stay in bed.

Guess what? Counting is NOT supposed to be used for this problem. Counting is more for controlling obnoxious behavior. Going to bed and staying there is basically a positive behavior that has to be encouraged with other tactics. Where would we find those strategies?

We had to finish reading the *1-2-3 Magic* book! We had been so delighted with the results of counting that we hadn't gone any further. There was a separate chapter called "Going to Bed—And Staying There!" There we learned The Basic Bedtime method. First we had to pick a bedtime and stick with it. Then, one-half hour before bedtime, we would inform Lucy that it was time to get ready for bed. She had to do everything to get ready and then check in with one of us. However much time was left in the half hour was story time or just one-on-one talking time. Then it would be lights out.

What about her getting up all the time? Some kids keep getting up because they don't want the fun of the day to end. Others get up because they're scared. The "cut them off at the pass" procedure would take care of either possibility.

Q&A ?

Questions for You

LUCY, DON'T YOU THINK IT'S TIME FOR BED?

NO.

List two mistakes Dad is making right here.

1. _____

2. _____

What are the two main reasons kids don't like to go to bed or stay in bed?

1. _____

2. _____

Questions for You

If you have a spouse or partner, what effects does child discipline have on your relationship?

_____

_____

_____

Why are the parents in this scene getting mad
at each other?

_____

_____

Questions for You

What would Mom like to say in this scene?

_____

_____

What would happen if Mom did say
something here?

_____

_____

_____

Sympathetic Listening

A big piece of Parenting Job #3, Strengthening Your Relationship with Your Children, is listening to what your kids have to say. You want to be a good listener when your children are happy and excited, but it's also important to be there for them when they're frustrated, sad or upset.

Unfortunately, Sympathetic Listening is easier to describe than it is to do. Sometimes we don't have the time to listen. At other times, however, we simply don't remember to take the time when we really could.

In our next story, **The Case of the Fickle Friends**, you will see me mishandle a situation in which my son was temporarily upset with some of his neighborhood buddies. In the portion of the story called the **WRONG WAY**, you'll see me being a lousy listener. In **THINKING IT THROUGH**, we'll take a look at what I messed up, Then we'll give you a chance to evaluate your own listening skills with your kids.

Finally, the **RIGHT WAY** section of our narrative will give me a chance to undo my mistake—an opportunity that doesn't always happen in real life!

THE CASE OF THE FICKLE FRIENDS

When my wife and I got our first house, we were thrilled to death. Not only did we have our own yard, but our kids would also have friends to play with. What wasn't so thrilling, however, was our introduction to the new and unfamiliar world of playtime politics.

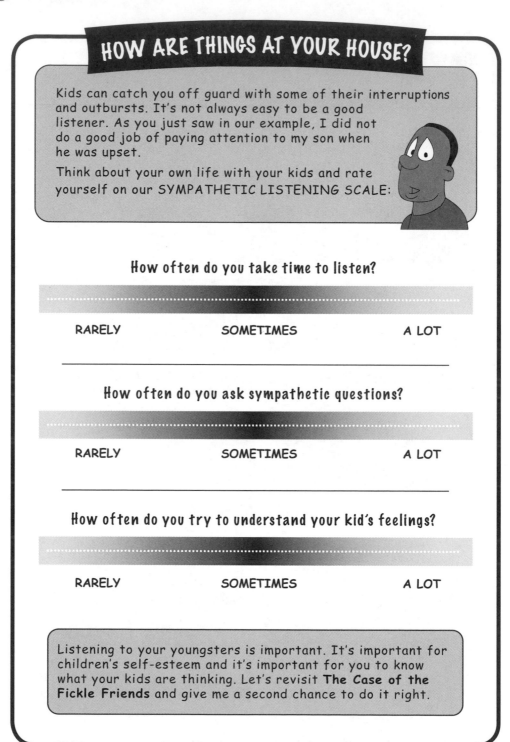

HOW ARE THINGS AT YOUR HOUSE?

Kids can catch you off guard with some of their interruptions and outbursts. It's not always easy to be a good listener. As you just saw in our example, I did not do a good job of paying attention to my son when he was upset.

Think about your own life with your kids and rate yourself on our SYMPATHETIC LISTENING SCALE:

How often do you take time to listen?

RARELY   SOMETIMES   A LOT

How often do you ask sympathetic questions?

RARELY   SOMETIMES   A LOT

How often do you try to understand your kid's feelings?

RARELY   SOMETIMES   A LOT

Listening to your youngsters is important. It's important for children's self-esteem and it's important for you to know what your kids are thinking. Let's revisit **The Case of the Fickle Friends** and give me a second chance to do it right.

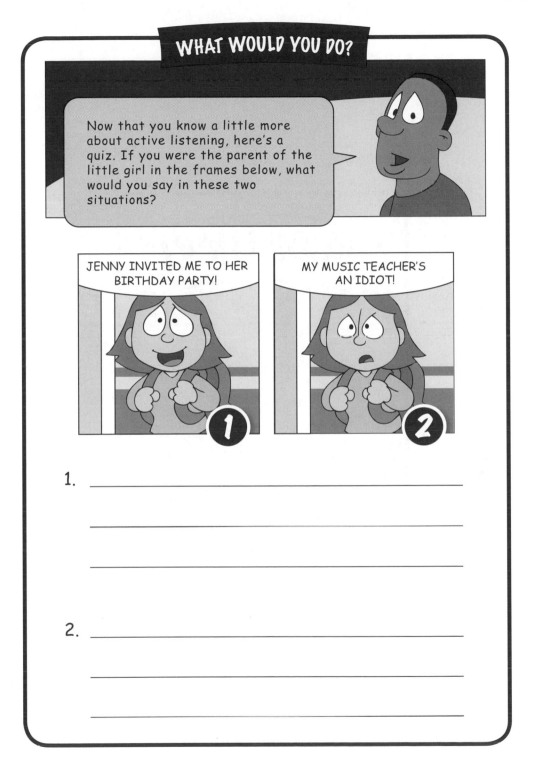

1. _____

_____

_____

2. _____

_____

_____

APPENDIX: Further Readings and Resources

Emotional Intelligence

• *Building Moral Intelligence: The Seven Essential Virtues That Teach Kids to Do the Right Thing.* Michele Borba, Ed.D. Jossey-Bass, 2002.

• *Emotional Intelligence: Why It Can Matter More than IQ.* Daniel Goleman, Bantam Books, 1995.

Active Listening and Problem Solving

• *Between Parent and Child.* Haim Ginott. Revised and Updated by Dr. Alice Ginott and Dr. H. Wallace Goddard. Three Rivers Press, 2003.

• *How to Talk So Kids Will Listen and Listen So Kids Will Talk.* Adele Faber and Elaine Mazlish. HarperCollins, 2004.

• *I Can Problem Solve: An Interpersonal Cognitive Problem-Solving Program.* Myrna B. Shure. Research Press, 2001.

Childhood Emotional Problems

• *The Emotional Problems of Normal Children: How Parents Can Understand and Help.* Stanley Turecki, M.D. with Sarah Warnick, Ph.D. Bantam Books, 1994.

• *Freeing Your Child from Anxiety: Powerful, Practical Solutions to Overcome Your Child's Fears, Worries, and Phobias.* Tamar E. Chansky. Broadway, 2004.

Separation and Divorce

• *The Unexpected Legacy of Divorce.* Judith Wallerstein, Julia M. Lewis and Sandra Blakeslee. Hyperion, 2000.

• *Co-Parenting After Divorce: How to Raise Happy, Healthy Children in Two-Home Families.* Winspeed Press, 2000.

Tech and Media

• www.wiredsafety.com *(Internet safety site)*

• www.netsmartz.org *(Very popular safety site used by educators, law enforcement and parents)*

• www.internetsafety.com *(Safe Eyes Internet filter)*

• www.commonsensemedia.org *(One-stop shop for reviews on TV, movies, music, games, books and websites – excellent resource)*

• www.webwatcherkids.com *(Information on monitoring software)*

Parenting Styles

• *Playful Parenting.* Lawrence J. Cohen, Ph.D. Ballantine, 2002.

• *The Power of Loving Discipline.* Karen Miles. Penguin, 2006.

• *The Anger Habit in Parenting.* Carl Semmelroth, Ph.D. Sourcebooks, Inc. 2005.

Child Temperament

• *Understanding Your Child's Temperament.* William B. Carey, M.D. Xlibris Corporation, 2004.

• *Temperament Tools: Working with Your Child's Inborn Traits*, Helen Neville and Diane Clark Johnson. Parenting Press, 1997.

Other Discipline Alternatives

• *Setting Limits with Your Strong-Willed Child: Eliminating Conflict by Establishing Clear, Firm, and Respectful Boundaries.* Robert J. MacKenzie. Three Rivers Press, 2001.

• *Have a New Kid by Friday! How to Change Your Child's Attitude, Behavior & Character in 5 Days.* Kevin Leman. Revell, 2008.

Research on *1-2-3 Magic*

• *Brief Psychoeducational Parenting Program: An Evaluation and 1-Year Followup.* Susan Bradley et al. Journal of the American Academy of Child and Adolescent Psychiatry, 42:10, October, 2003.

• *Authoritative Guide to Self-Help Resources in Mental Health.* John C. Norcross et al. Guilford Press, New York, 2003, pages 136, 139

• *Self-administered psychosocial treatments for children and families.* Frank J. Elgar, Patrick J. McGrath. Journal of Clinical Psychology, Vol. 59 (3), 321-339, 2003

• *Enhancing behavioral and social skill functioning in children newly diagnosed with Attention Deficit/Hyperactivity Disorder in a pediatric setting.* Steve Tutty, M.A., et al. Developmental and Behavioral Pediatrics, Vol.24, No.1, February, 2003.

• *Successful Methods for Increasing and Improving Parent and Child Interactions.* Jane Drapeaux. Paper Presented at the National Head Start Association 24th Annual Training Conference, May 25-31, 1997, Boston, Massachusetts.

• *1-2-3 Magic Part I: Its effectiveness on parental function in child discipline with preschool children.* Yeganeh Salehpour. Dissertation Abstracts International Section A: Humanities & Social Sciences. 57 (3-A), Sept 1996.